'The message of this fascinating and important book is that each of us is an embodied presence. We are used to the idea, of course, that all of our experience and conduct – our thoughts and feelings, our communications to, and with, others, and so on – are sourced in our personhood. That point is familiar to us. But we are definitely not used to the idea that our personhood, in turn, is a manifestation of body life. Merleau-Ponty had this crucial perspective; and now psychoanalysis will, too.'

Donnel Stern, *William Alanson White Institute and NYU Postdoctoral Program in Psychotherapy and Psychoanalysis*

'This highly accessible and engaging work is crucial for anyone interested in understanding the centrality of the body in psychoanalysis today. Drawing on a depth of clinical experience, Brothers and Sletvold introduce a new language for embodied therapeutic practice. In place of traditional concept-based theorizing, they develop a body-based approach that bridges the clinical, social and philosophical realms of experience. Brothers and Sletvold demonstrate just how fundamental our bodily being is to all that we do and experience in life. A timely and very welcome book that is an enrichment to our field.'

Roger Frie, *Simon Fraser University and the William Alanson White Institute of Psychiatry, Psychoanalysis and Psychology*

'Advocating for an embodied psychoanalysis, Brothers and Sletvold encourage clinicians and supervisors to expand the boundaries of the "talking cure" by attending to their own bodily experiences as well as those of their patients and supervisees. In original and clear language, they illustrate the transformative potential in clinical work of being grounded in the body. Whether in the consulting room or in political discourse, ethical practice requires that bodily vulnerability be acknowledged, owned, and processed, rather than dissociated or projected. Attending to our embodied experience and acknowledging our own vulnerability may help us become more attuned to our shared humanity.'

Karen Starr, *faculty at the NYU Postdoctoral Program in Psychotherapy and Psychoanalysis, co-editor of* Relational Psychoanalysis and Psychotherapy Integration *(2015), co-author of* A Psychotherapy for the People *(2013), and author of* Repair of the Soul *(2008)*

'For centuries, psychoanalysis has been described as "the talking cure" between one mind and another. In this book, Doris Brothers and Jon Sletvold bring "talking bodies" into the psychoanalytic conversation and treatment process. Framing their book within a contemporary "turn toward embodiment," a turn that to my mind has been all too slow in coming, the authors bring bodily experience and expression – in both defense and communication – back into the domain of psychoanalysis. Theirs is no easy task, but they break new ground in articulating a model of psychoanalysis deeply grounded in the somatic experiences of patients and analysts alike. Such central psychoanalytic concepts as trauma, transference, countertransference, memory and resistance are reconsidered through somatic lenses. Brothers and Sletvold present therapeutic and supervisory models of sustained attention to bodily processes that seek to reestablish a more vital flow of contact and communication between I, you, we, and world.'

William F. Cornell, *author of* Somatic Experience in Psychoanalysis and Psychotherapy

A New Vision of Psychoanalytic Theory, Practice and Supervision

By viewing psychoanalysis through the lens of embodiment, Brothers and Sletvold suggest a shift away from traditional concept-based theory and offer new ways to understand traumatic experiences, to describe the therapeutic exchange and to enhance the supervisory process.

Since traditional psychoanalytic language does not readily lend itself to embodied experience, the authors place particular emphasis on the words *I*, *you*, *we* and **world** to describe the flow of human attention. Offering new insights into trauma, this book demonstrates how traumatic experiences and efforts to regain certainty in one's psychological life involve profound disruptions of this flow. With a new understanding of transference, resistance and interpretation, the authors ultimately show how much can be gained from viewing the analytic exchange as a meeting between foreign bodies.

Grounded in detailed case material, this book will change the way therapists from all disciplines understand the therapeutic process and how viewing it in terms of talking bodies enhances their efforts to heal.

Doris Brothers is a co-founder of the Training and Research in Intersubjective Self Psychology Foundation. She serves on the council of the International Association for Psychoanalytic Self Psychology and has previously published three books, including *Toward a Psychology of Uncertainty: Trauma-Centered Psychoanalysis*. She practices in New York and Oslo.

Jon Sletvold is the founding board director of the Norwegian Character Analytic Institute. He has published books and articles on the role of the body in psychoanalysis and psychotherapy. He is the author of *The Embodied Analyst: From Freud and Reich to Relationality* (2014), winner of the Gradiva Award in 2015.

A New Vision of Psychoanalytic Theory, Practice and Supervision

TALKING BODIES

Doris Brothers and Jon Sletvold

Routledge
Taylor & Francis Group

LONDON AND NEW YORK

Designed cover image: Gustav Vigeland, *Sitting Man and Woman with Touching Foreheads*, 1916. Granite. Photo: Vigeland Museum.

First published 2023
by Routledge
4 Park Square, Milton Park, Abingdon, Oxon OX14 4RN

and by Routledge
605 Third Avenue, New York, NY 10158

Routledge is an imprint of the Taylor & Francis Group, an informa business

British Library Cataloguing-in-Publication Data
A catalogue record for this book is available from the British Library

ISBN: 978-1-032-20748-3 (hbk)
ISBN: 978-1-032-20749-0 (pbk)
ISBN: 978-1-003-26504-7 (ebk)

DOI: 10.4324/9781003265047

Typeset in Garamond
by Apex CoVantage, LLC

Contents

Acknowledgements   viii

Bodies in time: An introduction   1

1   Embodied language and the silence between the words   9

2   Foreign bodies: from interpretation to translation   20

3   Traumatized bodies   27

4   Embodying dissociation   40

5   Memory, narrative and the embodiment of transference   48

6   Resistance or the lack of freedom to change?   55

7   The us-them binary of fascist experience   68

8   Body-based supervision   78

9   Why not the body?   87

Coda   96
Appendix A   *The patient's perception of the analyst*   97
Appendix B   *Some past and present views on embodiment*   110
Index   120

Acknowledgements

We have had the immense good fortune to have written this book with the support and encouragement of a great many of our colleagues, friends, and relatives. Our children and grandchildren have surrounded us with love even though we have had to content ourselves with their on-screen images much of the time.

We are especially grateful for the deepening friendships we formed with the extraordinary people who joined our IAPSP support group at the onset of the COVID epidemic: Jill Gardner, Annette Richard, Dan Perlitz, Margy Sperry, and Judy Zevin.

The ideas in the book were test-driven in our supervision study groups on embodiment. Deep thanks go to Diane Bachman, Brian Buczynski, Diane Fremont, Grete Laine, Teodor Negulescu, Ramona Popescu, Vincent Stephen, Alexandra Tenebroso, and Georges Tremblay for their open-hearted contributions to what we have for called our "transatlantic group."

We are indebted to our Chinese colleagues Li Xin, Xu Jun 徐钧, and Zhang Jing 张静 for organizing presentations and supervisory groups for us, Chen Wei Chen 陈威辰 and Ji Li 吉莉 for their excellent work as translators, and to the many Chinese therapists who presented their work for embodied supervision and raised important questions about our approach.

Adrienne Harris has made it possible for us to present our work at the Ferenczi Center of the New School. Her insightful discussions and our dialogues with participants have added richly to several of the book's chapters.

We greatly appreciate the kind invitations by Jane Ryan, the inimitable creator of Confer, and Alice Jacobs Waterfall, Confer's content director, to present workshops and courses for Confer as well as the support of Josh Daniel, Shanida Osakonor, Claudia Roncallo, and Lucy Sam.

Our work has greatly benefitted from our presentations and discussions at the Norwegian Character Analytic Institute.

We are very grateful for the guidance and support of Kate Hawes, our superb Routledge Editor, and the expert help of the editorial assistant, Georgina Clutterbuck.

This book could not have been written without the trust and commitment of our patients. It has been during the course of our embodied conversations with them that we have developed the ideas that fill these pages.

Bodies in time

An introduction

What changes when we view psychoanalytic theory from the lens of embodiment? Nothing – and everything! While there is no disputing the enduring relevance of the concepts that have become known as interpretation, dissociation, transference and resistance, we believe that they are radically transformed when a body-based approach replaces traditional concept-based theorizing. In this book we attempt to illuminate these transformations by showing how our bodies and those of our patients "talk" to one another – sometimes with words and sometimes without them – and that our conversations are always affected by the world.

We believe that a "turn" toward embodiment is gaining momentum in our field, undoubtedly spurred by the rising influence of research in neuroscience and infant development. In the hope of contributing to this turn, we describe an approach to embodiment that makes use of some of the ideas each of us began to develop before we met.

When analysts focus on embodiment, they tend to become more aware of what is going on in the present moment. But we doubt that what is happening at any given moment is ever experienced as pure embodied sensation. Rather, we suspect that every present moment is saturated with meanings from the past and imbued with expectations for the future. In what follows, we sketch relevant bits of our past lives, our present situation and, if you read our book, some of what the near future holds for you.

Past – how we came together

Doris Brothers' story

Having contracted most of the known childhood illnesses and a few more serious diseases before I turned eight, I was often confined to my bed in the little Bronx, New York apartment I shared with my parents. Being a child who was happy with indoor activities, especially drawing, painting and reading, I cannot say that I missed the rollicking outdoor play my age-mates enjoyed. But the year I turned eight my body was released from its invisible

DOI: 10.4324/9781003265047-1

cocoon. Enrolled in after-school classes at Eileen Porwick's School of Dance, the enchantments of ballet, tap and acrobatics were suddenly revealed to me.

My infatuation with dance all but ended when I was ten, with my family's move to a part of Queens (another borough in New York City) that had no dance schools. Yet, when I think of how my interest in embodiment began, I recall how transformative those dance classes were. I can vividly remember the exquisite joy of moving to the rhythms my teachers coaxed out of the decrepit upright piano in the studio. I came wholly alive in ways that are hard to describe.

Although I cannot remember a time when I was not interested in the world of human relations, my path to becoming a psychologist and psychoanalyst was hardly the usual one. After attending a special high school for art and design, I had a very short stint as a fashion designer and then an advertising copywriter before deciding to devote myself to the study of clinical psychology. Like many people in our field, I discovered that what led me to enter psychoanalytic treatment were my childhood traumas. During the 12 years of what was a profoundly life-changing analytic relationship, I became aware of the ways in which these traumas had affected me.

As a young student of psychology, my interest in movement and my dim awareness that psychological life was profoundly tied to embodiment led me to Jacob Moreno's workshops in psychodrama and Kathy Stilson's classes in improvisational theater. Yet, I rarely considered the bodily bases of human psychology during my time in graduate school at Yeshiva University, or even when I helped to establish a self-psychological training institute. It was trauma that almost totally absorbed my interest. In 1988 I was fortunate to collaborate with Richard Ulman in writing *The Shattered Self: A Psychoanalytic Study of Trauma*. Some of the ideas we developed in that book have remained important to me to this day, although I have continually reworked them. These include the idea that trauma does not reside in an event alone but in its subjective meaning, and that traumatic experiences invariably lead to restorative efforts.

In my next book, *Falling Backwards: A Study of Trust and Self Experience*, published in 1995, I drew on my experiences with rape and incest survivors during my work for Women Against Rape and my dissertation on trust disturbances in this traumatized population. The book locates betrayals of various kinds of trust at the heart of trauma. Soon after the book was published, I came to realize that trust was necessary and its betrayal devastating because we cannot be certain that the relationships necessary for psychological existence will be available; we can only trust that they will be. I subsequently examined the experience of traumatic uncertainty in a book entitled *Toward a Psychology of Uncertainty: Trauma-Centered Psychoanalysis*.

It was almost immediately after submitting the manuscript of that book to the publisher in 2008 that I realized that I had neglected two crucially important aspects of trauma: its intergenerational transmission as reflected in our cultural, political, historical situatedness and the fact that trauma profoundly disrupts our bodily functioning. Although I was able to speculate in a journal article (Brothers, 2014) about the transmission of trauma from one generation to the next by using attachment theory, my efforts to convey what I felt were the bodily effects of trauma were frustratingly unsuccessful. In Lynne Jacobs' combination of gestalt theory and relational psychoanalysis, and in the movement workshops I took with Ruella Frank, I gained glimmers of what I was searching for. But it was not until I read articles that Jon Sletvold published in 2011 and 2012 that I found the approach to embodiment that jibed with my psychoanalytic perspective.

In Jon's writings, I discovered that therapists and patients convey their traumatic experiences from body to body in ways that cannot be communicated verbally. Not only is it possible for therapists to gain some understanding of their patients' suffering through automatic imitation, but they communicate this understanding to their patients.

Jon's writings on embodied supervision were particularly meaningful for me insofar as they demonstrated that by feeling themselves into their patients' bodies and re-experiencing their own bodily reactions in relation to them, therapists discover what had caused therapeutic impasses and misunderstandings. This approach allows therapists to become aware of how their own bodies carry traumatic meanings that may impede their work. No other perspective had allowed me to see how understanding the embodiment of trauma might change existing theory and treatment.

After Jon and I met at a conference in 2015 and subsequently began to talk about our work and therapeutic experiences, it gradually became clearer and clearer to the both of us that by combining our approaches we could develop a new psychoanalytic vision for our field.

Jon Sletvold's story

It is not clear what made me decide to study psychology during my last year in high school, since I had not yet even met a psychologist. When I made my decision, which I have never regretted, my only knowledge of psychology came from reading Freud's *Introductory Lectures in Psychoanalysis*. Despite my fascination with Freud's writings, particularly his focus on sexuality, I now realize that I was more interested in understanding what was going on between people than what was going on inside individuals.

As I think about my early life, I recall my great interest in what I took to be conflicts and difficulties in neighboring families and my reluctance to focus on the problems I experienced within my own family – especially those that were traumatizing. This probably explains why, during my student years, I studied social psychology and its applied branches like organizational and industrial psychology.

It was only after being hired to teach social psychology, and encountering students who were more interested in clinical psychology and psychotherapy, that I too decided to become a clinician. I had avoided any in-depth study of psychoanalysis, which at that time (around 1970), seemed to consist mostly of ego psychology, a theory that did not appeal to me. However, I welcomed the opportunity to study Rogerian Client-Centered therapy. I said farewell to social psychology by delivering a dissertation criticizing statistics-based social psychology experiments for being unable to produce accumulated knowledge.

In Kohut's self-psychology, I found a psychoanalytic perspective that appealed to me because, like Rogers' client-centered therapy, it focused on empathy and relationships. It was, however, only after encountering Mitchell's *Relational Concepts in Psychoanalysis* (1988) that I found a version of psychoanalysis that resonated completely with my own psychological sensibility.

As a young psychologist, I had no specific ideas about trauma and traumatic experiences. It did not seem to have a prominent place in psychology and psychiatry in the 1970s. Nevertheless, my interest in what was going on between people made it natural for me to look for the roots of my patient's difficulties in events in their lives, events that I later learned to term "traumas."

What I hope to convey is that my interest in traumatic experiences dates back far longer than my professional interest in the body. However, towards the end of the 70s, an interest in the role of the body in psychotherapy gradually developed, starting with the introduction of relaxation techniques. In 1987, I was invited to participate in a training in the Pesso Boyden System Psychomotor Therapy (PBSP). This training combined my interest in human relationships and an in-depth focus on embodied experience, which suited me perfectly. I then decided to terminate the psychoanalytic training I had embarked on in favor of entering a training analysis with the character analyst, Nils Strand, and to pursuing training within the post-Reichian tradition in Norway. This became the start of my lifelong engagement with an embodied Reichian tradition, and my efforts to integrate it with the relational turn in psychoanalysis. I described this development in *The Embodied Analyst – From Freud and Reich to Relationality* (2014).

I gradually realized that my writings on embodiment lacked an explicit focus on traumatic experience. This led me to a study of Freud's views on trauma and to write an article entitled, "Freud's Three Theories of Neurosis: Towards a Contemporary Theory of Trauma and Defense" (2016). In this article, I argued that psychoanalysis should embrace Freud's initial trauma-based hypotheses regarding the cause of neurosis rather than his later theories about inborn conflicting drives. When I first met Doris Brothers in 2015, I learned that she had argued this position several decades earlier (Ulman & Brothers, 1988).

After reading Brothers' book, *Toward a Psychology of Uncertainty: Trauma-Centered Psychoanalysis* (2008), I realized that her theory of certainty/uncertainty captured what had been missing in my understanding of the consequences of traumatic experiences. I felt that Brothers' focus on the urgent need to establish a sense of certainty about psychological survival in the aftermath of traumatic experiences hit the nail on the head. And it resonated well with my embodied focus on body-rigidity or "muscular armor." Furthermore, Brothers' view of the therapeutic process as aimed at developing a greater tolerance for uncertainty felt deeply meaningful for me. It gave a new dimension and more clarity to my view of the centrality of our ability to keep both an embodied sense of ourselves and others in mind. Additionally, Brothers renewed my early interest in the psychological aspects and consequences of political upheavals in the world. A few years before we met, she had played a central role in putting on the psychoanalytic conference, *Bystanders No More*. A foundation was built for the close collaboration that has been developing between us ever since.

Present – where we are now

Having fallen in love, a thoroughly embodied phenomenon, we married in December of 2021. At present we live and work together in Oslo and New York.

We also believe that we are presently living in the midst of a remarkable turn in our field that restores embodiment to its rightful place at the center of the psychoanalytic project. This idea has been confirmed by the contributions to an issue of *Psychoanalytic Inquiry* (2021, 42:4) that we co-edited, entitled "The Turn Toward Embodiment." It features articles by Donnel Stern, Siri Gullestad, William Cornell, Steven Knoblauch, Gianni Nebbiosi and Susi Federici as well as us. See Appendix B for a brief review of some of the work on embodiment that was done in past eras as well as some that are transforming psychoanalysis today.

Near future – what you will find in this book

In Chapter 1 we suggest a shift away from a word-and-concept-based psychoanalysis to one that is fundamentally body-based. Drawing on the work of Merleau-Ponty and Lakoff and Johnson, we provide a rationale for using the words *I, you, we* and **world** in place of traditional psychoanalytic language – whenever possible – in order to allow analysts to feel what is being conveyed in their bodies. We contend that while our attention tends to move among these aspects of mind, many factors affect the fluidity and ease of the *I-you-we-world* flow.

We then offer a new approach for describing clinical situations based on this suggested language. This involves selecting a critical moment in the therapeutic exchange and first focusing on one's own bodily reactions to a patient, then "becoming" the patient through imitation, and finally visualizing the interaction between oneself and the patient.

We conclude the chapter by discussing what happens in "the silence between the words." It is in this silence that bodies do a great deal of talking.

We devote Chapter 2 to an idea that is central to our approach, namely that psychoanalytic encounters take place between "foreign bodies." Contending that interactions between foreign bodies require translation, we suggest replacing the traditional translational mode – interpretation – with the forms of translation suggested by contemporary translation theorists. Two clinical illustrations are presented, one involving a woman patient who, at first, seemed very similar to Doris, and one involving a woman patient who, at first, seemed very different from Jon.

We develop the idea that traumatizing experiences involve massive disruptions to the complex intertwining of *I, you, we,* and *world* in Chapter 3. Our model challenges some of the prevailing ideas about the concept of trauma that are closely linked to the familiar PTSD model.

We provide an alternative understanding of dissociation by explaining how the need to simplify experience in trauma's aftermath often leads to the slowing or freezing of the *I-you-we-world* flow. We describe the development of *I*-centeredness, *you*-centeredness and **we**-centeredness as well as the creation of binaries as consequences of the slowed or frozen flow. Our understanding of the differences between early-life and adult-onset traumas, as well as our ideas about the ways in which imagination is used in the aftermath of trauma, is illustrated through clinical examples.

Chapter 4 explores the similarities and differences between our view of dissociation and what we call "the dissociation-enactment model" that is closely associated with the work of Philip Bromberg and Donnel Stern, among other relational analysts. We contend that although the dissociation-enactment model represents a step toward an embodied understanding of dissociation, it maintains a conceptual split between embodied dyadic interaction on the one hand and the internal mind on the other. We also object to the use of the term, "enactment," insofar as it emphasizes past traumas and downplays the ways the bodies of the analytic couple talk about trauma in the here and now. We also provide an alternative to the widely accepted notion of "multiple-self states."

According to our understanding, dissociation results from the traumatic breakdown of *I-you-we-world* such that one of these experiential components comes to dominate conscious awareness. A detailed clinical example, involving a patient who suffered from extreme forms of dissociation in which she "heard" voices, illustrates some of our ideas.

While dissociative forgetting is often cited as the hallmark of trauma, in Chapter 5 we try to show that memories – both verbal-declarative and nonverbal-implicit – play an equally crucial role. Building on the idea that memory is narrative in nature, and the importance of memory in Freud's understanding of transference, we revisit the concept of transference. In our view, it is only when traumatic memories have slowed the flow of *I, you, we* and *world* that specific transferences can be identified. A clinical example involving the bodily manifestation of traumatic experiences for both analyst and patient is presented.

In Chapter 6, we examine a possible reason for the wrenching difficulty so often encountered in attaining therapeutic change: desirable as it might seem to be, the sense of being free to change, a necessary component of agency, is often experienced as terrifyingly fraught with danger. This conceptualization has led us to offer an alternative understanding of what has been termed, "resistance." Drawing on Roger Frie's understanding that agency is fundamentally embodied, we attempt to show that the fear of therapeutic change may be alleviated or even eliminated through embodied connectedness, or the development of a sense of *we*-ness. An illustrative clinical example is offered.

We then explore the lack of freedom to change experienced by patients whose constitutional make-up includes what we call "subtle neurological conditions" such as ADHD and high-functioning autism. Through clinical illustrations we try to show the intertwining of trauma with these conditions insofar as they too involve disruptions to the *I-you-we-world* flow.

In Chapter 7, we examine the trauma-generated binary of "us and them," which lies at the heart of fascist experience. We emphasize the crucial distinction between a *we* that is based on *I* and *you,* and a *we* without a *you.* Looking back to Wilhelm Reich's prescient understanding of fascist experience, we suggest that being human involves being vulnerable to experiencing this ubiquitous binary. Each of us then describes how we were caught up in the *us-them* binary in relation to patients who supported fascistic leaders.

We conclude the chapter by showing how the us-them binary affects psychoanalytic organizations and practice.

Chapter 8 is devoted to the model of embodied supervision that we have been using in our work with several groups of clinicians. We explain how this model, which has evolved from the work of Jon and his colleagues at the Norwegian Character Analytic Institute, differs from traditional psychoanalytic supervision. In contrast to traditional supervision, which locates knowledge and authority in the supervisor, we believe that clinical knowledge and authority reside in the bodies of the supervisees and their patients. We hope to show how the supervisory positions of *I, you* and *we* resemble the positions we use in our clinical illustrations. By including the contributions of members of our groups, we add *world* to the supervisory process.

We present supervisory sessions that we have conducted with two therapists in what we have come to call our "transatlantic group" and a therapist in one of our Chinese groups.

Chapter 9, our concluding chapter, attempts to answer the question, "Why has psychoanalysis been so slow in recognizing the importance of embodiment?" We begin with the idea that people in the western world are often confused about their relationships to their bodies. We provide Sam Anderson's entertaining as well as insightful exploration of the possible ways in which humans may experience their embodiment.

We suggest that Freud's reliance on the energy-discharge science of his time, which proved to be largely incompatible with contemporary scientific thinking, may have delayed the development of a truly embodied psychoanalysis.

We then turn to the vexing problem of touch for analysts, which is steeped in the early history of psychoanalysis. We outline our concept of "skinship," by which we mean the experience of freedom shared by patients and therapists to touch (or not to touch) one another in nonsexual ways. Brief clinical examples are described.

We then present Zeynep Catay's research on what she calls "somatic countertransference." She describes the fears that lead therapists to avoid focusing on bodies.

The chapter ends with a consideration of the longing to transcend the body insofar as bodies confront analysts with their mortality and force them to become aware of differences in patients' physicality that they would prefer to ignore.

We conclude our book with a coda in which we describe ideas that readers may want to take with them.

The book has two appendices. In Appendix A, "The Patient's Perception of the Analyst," we offer insights by other analysts about the reason for the neglect of the patient's perception of the analyst as well as some examples in which these perceptions are highlights. We also present accounts by two of Freud's patients of their perceptions of him as well as an account by Erich Fromm's biographer of his perception of Fromm.

In Appendix B, "Some Past and Present Views on Embodiment," we offer brief accounts of the ways other analysts have emphasized embodiment in their work.

References

Brothers, D. (1995). *Falling backwards: An exploration of trust and self-experience*. New York: Norton.

Brothers, D. (2008). *Toward a psychology of uncertainty: Trauma-centered psychoanalysis*. New York: Psychoanalytic Inquiry Book Series, Analytic Press.

Brothers, D. (2014). Traumatic attachments: Intergenerational trauma, dissociation and the analytic relationship. *International Journal of Psychoanalytic Self Psychology, 9*(1), 3–15.

Brothers, D., & Ulman, R. B. (1988). *The shattered self: A psychoanalytic study of trauma*. Hillsdale, NJ: Analytic Press.

Mitchell, S. (1988). *Relational concepts in psychoanalysis*. Cambridge, MA: Harvard University Press.

Sletvold, J. (2011). The reading of emotional expression. Wilhelm reich and the history of embodied analysis. *Psychoanalytic Dialogues, 21*, 453–467.

Sletvold, J. (2012). Training analysts to work with unconscious embodied expressions. *Psychoanalytic Dialogues, 22*, 410–429.

Sletvold, J. (2014). *The embodied analyst – From freud and reich to relationality*. London and New York: Routledge Taylor & Frances.

Sletvold, J. (2016). Freud's three theories of neurosis: Towards a contemporary theory of trauma and defense. *Psychoanalytic Dialogues, 26*, 460–475. DOI: 10.1080/10481885.1190611.

Chapter 1

Embodied language and the silence between the words[1]

We cannot help wondering how Freud would have reacted to the title of our book. Would he have exploded with anger at the audacious idea that his celebrated brainchild needed a new vision? Or would he have smiled encouragingly, content that psychoanalysis was finally on track to fully realize its mission? Of course, we have no way of knowing what his reactions might have been, or even if he would have been moved to react at all. Still, we write this book in the fond hope that we are in some small way contributing to the evolution of Freud's profound and enduring insights.

We begin by explaining what we mean by a new vision of psychoanalytic theory, practice and supervision. By no means do we intend to invent a new form of psychoanalysis. Rather what we have in mind involves taking a fresh look, viewing psychoanalysis from a perspective that reveals what has always been there. While psychoanalysis has traditionally taken words and concepts as its starting point, we contend that embodied experience is its ground zero. As Freud (1923) famously wrote: "The ego is first and foremost a bodily ego." Even earlier in his career Freud (1890) observed:

> A man's states of mind are manifested, almost without exception, in the tensions and relaxations of his facial muscles, in the adaptations of his eyes, in the amount of blood in the vessels of his skin, in the modifications in his vocal apparatus and in the movements of his limbs and in particular of his hands.
>
> (S.E. VII, p. 286)

Another early analyst who suggested that patients not only talk with words but with their whole bodies was Wilhelm Reich. He observed that "the patient's behaviour (manner, look, language, countenance, dress, handshake, etc.) not only is vastly underestimated in terms of its analytic importance but is usually completely overlooked" (Reich, 1933/49/72, p. 31).

What we would add to these pioneering observations is that what we see in our patients' bodies always reflects their ongoing conversations with others'

DOI: 10.4324/9781003265047-2

bodies; bodies are always talking to one another (see Appendix B for a review of writings on embodiment by other writers).

We suggest a shift away from a word-and-concept-based psychoanalysis to one that is fundamentally body-based. Words and concepts still play a vital, even indispensable role in our work. However, as we explain in greater detail shortly, like Lakoff and Johnson (1999), we consider concepts, even the most abstract, as rooted in bodily interactions among people and with their environment. We have often noticed that especially relevant – and, at times, beautiful – images and concepts enter the psychoanalytic dialogue when analysts focus on their own and their patients' embodied feelings.

It is our basic assumption that whatever enters our minds has already affected our bodies (Spinoza,1677/1982; Merleau-Ponty, 1945; Damasio, 1994; Sletvold, 2014). From this embodied perspective, psychoanalytic therapy is seen as a continuing process of perceiving, sensing and feeling what is happening in our bodies as we interact.

Finding words

We believe that we have identified one of the main reasons that embodiment cannot be fully understood from the vantage point of existing psychoanalytic theory: traditional psychoanalytic language does not easily lend itself to embodied experience. That is, it consists of words or phrases that do not readily allow readers or speakers to feel the meaning of what is communicated in their bodies. Some common examples of concept-based language are such widely used terms as "intersubjectivity," "object relations," "the field," "the third" and "mentalization." While we recognize the need to use such words and concepts in certain contexts in order to communicate complex ideas, we believe that they sometimes obscure the human experiences they intend to explicate.

Several analysts have already tried to develop a more experience-near language for psychoanalysis. Roy Schafer's attempt in *A New Language for Psychoanalysis* (1976) is one outstanding example. We consider his effort to replace traditional psychoanalytic concepts with action language to be a step towards a body-based psychoanalysis. George Klein's work also pointed in this direction. He (Klein, 1976) argued that Freud's metapsychological theory ought to be replaced with his more experience-near clinical theory. In our view, however, both Schafer's and Klein's efforts were limited by their adherence to classical psychoanalytic ideas that prevailed prior to the relational turn.

We also realize that to work in the profound uncertainty that pervades our therapeutic relationships, analysts tend to take comfort in using traditional words that are known and familiar. Nevertheless, we believe that if analysts fully acknowledge their embodied humanness, using language that ignores or invalidates this inescapable reality runs counter to their mission.

Our efforts to find language that connects us more closely with bodily experience find support in the philosophical writings of Maurice Merleau-Ponty. As Dillon (1997) observes, a fundamental idea remains constant throughout Merleau-Ponty's treatment of language:

> Language comes into being within the phenomenal world and could not exist without it or *the human bodies interacting within it*. Language is thus a founded phenomenon, a phenomenon founded upon human embodiment within the world and must be understood within this context.
>
> (M.C. Dillon, 1997, p. 186, italics added)

We find inspiration in Merleau-Ponty's references to the bodily gesture as necessary for bridging the gap between prelinguistic and linguistic phases in the evolution of speech among humans. He claimed that sounds and gestures emanating from human bodies are intrinsically meaningful. Arguing against the idea advanced by de Saussure that the relation of signifier to signified is arbitrary, Merleau-Ponty (1964, p. 187) explained that the conceptual and delimiting meaning of words would no longer appear arbitrary "if we took into account the emotional content of the word, which we have called . . . its 'gestural' sense, which is all important in poetry, for example."

It is very much the emotional content of the words we use both in psychoanalytic writing and in our work as therapists, teachers and supervisors that we hope to place in the foreground. We believe that Merleau-Ponty's notion of language as "singing the world" captures this idea. Consider this passage from *Signs*:

> Words, vowels, and phonemes are so many ways of *singing the world*, and . . . their function is to represent things, not as the naïve onomatopoetic theory had it, by reason of an objective resemblance, but because they extract, and literally express, their emotional essence.
>
> (1960, *Signs* p. 120, emphasis added)

Our view is also highly congruent with the work of Lakoff and Johnson (1980, 1999), who developed the notion that semantics emerges from the experience of the body interacting with the environment. In their book, *Metaphors We Live By* (1980), they not only demonstrate the prevalence of metaphors in everyday language but also that our ordinary conceptual system, in terms of which we both think and act, is fundamentally metaphorical and body-based in nature. Consider this example: the concept *relieved* refers to letting go of an emotional burden but is derived from the feeling of the body getting rid of a physical burden. Another example is touch. We may refer to something as "touching" when it is emotionally affecting but touching also means being so close to something that it makes contact.

Lakoff and Johnson began their book, *Philosophy in the Flesh*, with three statements that we endorse: (1) mind is inherently embodied, (2) thought is mostly unconscious and (3) abstract concepts are largely metaphorical (Lakoff & Johnson (1999, p. 3). The reason, they explain, is not based on abstract laws but is grounded in bodily experience

Influenced by their arguments, we have found that words common in everyday speech seem better suited to our goal of exchanging body-based communication for the prevailing concept-based language. So, we prefer the word, "I," to "ego" or "the self"; the word, "you," to "object"; and the word, "we;" to "object relations," "selfobject," "the third" or "the field."

We realize that no language that we use to describe our bodily sensing of ourselves, our sense of *I*, corresponds only to direct bodily experiencing. Although saying "I am in pain," rather than "I feel pain in my arm," indicates an awareness that a person and his or her body cannot be separated, the moment that we communicate *about* a feeling in our bodies, we experience ourselves as differentiated from our bodies to some extent.

We usually experience the knowing, explaining, analyzing, describing, observing *I* simultaneously with the *I* who is feeling. However, at times the knowing *I* is more in the foreground of our experience while the feeling *I* is more in the background, while at other times it is just the reverse. It is only during moments of extreme pain or extreme pleasure, such as during orgasm, that the knowing, explaining, analyzing *I* is entirely eclipsed by the feeling bodily *I*. And it is when we are dreaming or fantasizing or engrossed in reading or writing that a sense of the feeling *I* may be all but lost – even if what is on our minds is still the product of a living body. It is probably this double experiencing, reinforced by Western languages, that gave rise to Cartesian dualism. We imagine that only animals and newborns experience themselves exclusively in a bodily way.

Just as using the word *I* connects people with a bodily sense of themselves, so does using the word *you*. We believe this is so because of our innate capacity for automatic inner imitation (Sletvold, 2014, Nebbiosi & Federici, 2022). Freud was well aware of the power of imitation. He wrote:

> A path leads from identification by way of imitation to empathy, that is, to the comprehension of the mechanism by means of which we are enabled to take up any attitude at all towards another mental life.
>
> (Freud, 1921, p. 110, fn. 2)

And somewhat later, Wilhelm Reich suggested that:

> The patient's expressive movements involuntarily bring about an imitation in our own bodies by means of which we "sense" and understand the expression in ourselves and, consequently, in the patient.
>
> (Reich, 1933/49, p. 362)

More recently, research on mirror neurons (Gallese, 2009) and imitation in early infancy (Meltzoff & Decity, 2003) has given strong support to the view that we learn to know both ourselves and others, both *I* and *you*, by attending to the feeling of our bodies (Sletvold, 2014, Nebbiosi & Federici, 2008).

You have only to remember a dream to appreciate how easily we imitate other people in our lives. The characters who populate our dreams are often wonderfully exact replicas of others we have known. And, of course, the characters in novels, plays and films are created from the *you* experiences of their creators.

Siri Hustvedt (2010) observes: " 'I' exists only in relation to 'you' " (p. 55). It is while focusing on *you* that we are enabled to feel our passion for others – our love, our hate, our envy, our compassion, even our desire for revenge. We believe our humanness is largely the result of our capacity to feel ourselves into the bodies of others, our capacity for empathy. As we hope to demonstrate in Chapter 7, which we devote to embodied supervision, the capacity for embodied empathy can be developed.

One of the most important discoveries of the 20th century involves the idea that one's sense of self (*I*) cannot exist independent of a sense of one's connectedness with others (*you* and **we**). As far as we can tell, a sense of **we** emerges from the sensing of *I* and *you*.

The varieties of **we**-ness that exist among humans are probably limitless. The richness and complexity of one's sense of being connected to others depends on one's stage of development – an infant's sense of connectedness to caretakers is very different from what a mature adult feels with respect to a loved or hated other. Yes, a sense of **we** is often intensely experienced between adversaries. And how we experience **we**-ness is powerfully influenced by our life experiences – especially, as we shall see, our trauma histories. But perhaps most importantly, the quality of a sense of **we** depends on how one is met by others. And, one's constitutional strengths and weaknesses certainly play roles. We must also point out that the numbers of others included in a sense of **we** ranges from one other person, or even one nonhuman living creature or thing, to one's family, community, country, to God, even the entire world.

We want to point out that even if the words *I, you,* and **we** enable us to more easily contact our embodied experience, it is sometimes extremely awkward to use them descriptively on an explanatory level. Consequently, we will often use such words as "oneself," "the other" or "others," and "the feeling of connectedness" throughout the book to describe these experiences.

We hope we have not conveyed the idea that the only words that allow us to contact our bodily experience are *I, you* and **we**. Many words and phrases connect us with our bodies – think of the words used by poets. We can often identify patients who are fearful of emotional connectedness by their choice of concept-based language. However, even those who use body-based language may still avoid the depth of feelings their words suggest. The analyst's focus on their own and the patient's embodied communication hopefully makes for a more authentic feeling exchange.

We use the word "*world*" as a kind of shorthand to describe aspects of life that do not directly involve human relating such as nature, science, the arts, religion, spirituality, politics, etc.

I, you and *we* are steeped in and shaped by the world in which we live. Race, class, ethnicity, political orientation, sex, gender, sexual preference and the intangible elements of culture play profound roles in these elements of lived experience.

The concept of *world* is essential in Merleau-Ponty's understanding of language and history. Consider his thoughts about "the world's explosion within us":

> It is asked, "Where is history made? Who makes it? What is this movement which traces out and leaves behind the figures of the wake?" It is of the same order as the movement of Thought and Speech, and, in short, of *the perceptible world's explosion within us.* . . . We are in the field of history as we are in the field of language or existence.
>
> (Merleau-Ponty, 1964, p. 20, italics added)

We are hardly alone in emphasizing the importance of the world in psychoanalysis. Freud led the way. One outstanding example is *Thoughts for the Times on War and Death* (1915) that Freud wrote six months after the outbreak of World War I. In the books' two essays he describes his disillusionment with human nature as well as with the state's use of violence.

A book edited by Roger Frie and Pascal Sauvayre (2022) documents how the groundbreaking cross-disciplinary approach employed by early interpersonal psychoanalysts demonstrated the impact of social and political forces on human psychology. We cannot begin to mention all the many analytic writers who focus on history, politics and current events, but we are grateful for the ways they have broadened our perspective.

The *I-you-we-world* flow

We believe that most of human experiencing involves a flow of attention among the various components of the *I, you, we* and *world* totality. However, few, if any of us, are likely to shift attention from one component to another with effortless fluidity. The degree of ease or difficulty with which any given individual experiences the *I-you-we-world* flow is affected by many complex and overlapping factors including the individual's developmental level, constitutional makeup, relational surround, trauma history as well as the here-and-now context. Just how this flow develops, and perhaps declines, throughout the life span, requires investigation by developmental psychologists.

The complexity of the *I-you-we-world* flow is compounded by our understanding that the experience of *I-you-we-world* in one individual is continually affected by and affects the experience of *I-you-we-world* among all of the individual's relational partners. As we see it, this complex intermingling of *I-you-we-world* is maintained through body-to-body exchanges. In fact, we suggest that a sense of embodied wholeness is not possible outside of one's body-to-body connections with others. Although we need not be in close physical proximity with one another, to the extent that our interactions are feeling-laden, our exchanges are embodied.

Optimally, in the absence of trauma there would be a fluid, effortless shifting of awareness from one aspect of the intermingling, overlapping complexity of *I, you, we* and *world* to another. However, we are not convinced that humans have ever lived in a world free of trauma. Relational conflicts, wars and natural disasters pervade history. We see psychoanalytic treatment as aiming toward the fluid flow of *I-you-we-world* as it intermingles with the *I-you-we-world flow* of others. Yet, because of the ubiquity of traumatizing experiences, we realize that no one is likely to achieve such a flow completely, or to sustain it for very long.

In the face of strong emotional challenges and traumas, this complex interweaving of experience breaks down and our sense of embodied wholeness is fractured (we take up the effects of trauma on the intermingling flow of *I-you-we-world* in Chapter 2).

Consciousness and unconsciousness in the *I-you-we-world* flow

Freud's understanding of the prevalence of unconscious experience remains the cornerstone of psychoanalytic practice to this day. Wide support for the idea of unconsciousness is to be found in the work of many contemporary neuroscientists such as Damasio (1994, 2010). We believe that much of the *I-you-we-world* flow is unavailable to conscious awareness. While the feelings, fantasies and memories that attend our focus on any aspect of the *I-you-we-world* flow may continuously affect our lives, we may never become aware of all of them.

In the clinical situation, what is conscious in the intermingling *I-you-we-world* flow at any given moment for the analyst may not be the same for the patient and vice versa. Bodies "talk" about these experiences, even when they are not verbally shared. That is to say, facial expressions, gestures, tones of voice, etc., may communicate what is unavailable to consciousness for the analytic partners. However, we object to the idea that the analyst's attention to the way the patient's body "talks" reveals the truth about the patient's experience. After all, the analyst is continually monitoring bodily communications through his, her or their own *I-you-we-world* organization.

We find that the disparities between what is experienced consciously and unconsciously for both the patient and the analyst continuously affects the quality of their sense of *we*-ness. These disparities, which often result from dissociation in both or either therapeutic partner, are stirred by memories of past traumas (see Chapters 2, 3 and 4).

Describing the therapeutic process

Bodies do not talk to one another in the big-picture, concept-based language of psychoanalytic theory. They communicate in moment-to-moment exchanges much like those that are captured in Beatrice Beebe's descriptions of mother-infant interactions (Beebe & Lachmann, 2014). Our challenge in showing how an embodied perspective changes the clinical situation involves finding a way to convey the intermingling of the flow of *I-you-we-world* for the analyst and the patient. We are well aware that doing so necessarily means that we must artificially simplify aspects of the enormous complexity of the analytic exchange.

In the clinical examples that appear throughout this book, we begin by explaining the clinical situation in the familiar, descriptive language of countless psychoanalytic write-ups. We then turn to our model of embodied supervision as first outlined by Sletvold (2012, 2014) to illustrate our approach. In what we call "the *I* position," we zoom in on a specific moment in the therapeutic exchange. In this position, we first describe what we experienced when imagining ourselves to once again be with the patient during the selected time. We try to describe what we become aware of in our bodies as well as our thoughts and fantasies in as complete a way as possible. Next, in "the *you* position," we attempt to "become" our patient by imitating the patient's facial expressions, gestures, movements and his or her way of speaking. We describe what we have experienced in our bodies as well as feelings and thoughts that occur to us as we imitate the patient. Finally, in the "*we* position," we attempt to envision the exchange between ourselves and the patient by keeping in mind how we felt with the patient and how we felt when we imitated the patient. The clinical illustrations that we present in subsequent chapters will hopefully clarify our way of describing the therapeutic process.

The silence between the words – embodied stories

As we have tried to convey, we could not imagine conducting a therapeutic relationship, or any relationship for that matter, without words. But between the words that we utter and hear are silences that are never empty. They overflow with feeling-soaked meanings that can only be grasped by nonverbal means. It is in the silences between the words that bodies do much of their talking.

When bodies talk to one another, they sometimes shout their meanings. Who cannot grasp the meaning of bared teeth and clenched fists, of arms encircling another in a passionate embrace? But sometimes bodies speak so softly they seem to whisper their meanings. A raised eyebrow, a tightening of the jaw, an upturned palm, may easily go unnoticed and crucial information is lost. We have found that when students practice tuning into their own bodies and those of their patients, they learn to understand these changes in volume with ever greater facility (see Chapter 7).

We believe that what fills the silence between the words are narratives, or as we prefer to call them, stories. Bruner (1991), one of the most celebrated narrative theorists of our time, writes, "narrative . . . cannot in the jargon of narratology, be 'voiceless'" (p. 77). But this conviction has recently been challenged. Lichtenberg (2017), for example, has described the infant's "non-verbal narratives." He notes that, while in ordinary usage, narrative addresses verbal stories, he and his collaborators, Frank Lachmann and James Fosshage, broaden narrative to encompass the experience of imagistic, auditory, body movement and body sensation stories for both the preverbal infant and the individual throughout life.

Lichtenberg (2017, p. 9) notes that Daniel Stern's RIGs (Representations of Interactions that have been Generalized) are narratives, adding that "procedural memory is a narrative of what to do under particular circumstances." Moreover, he regards narrative as "embodied history." He contends that movement patterns and physiological sensations are comparable to symbolic representation. Citing Frank and LaBarre (2010), who identify fundamental movements such as yield, push, reach, grasp, pull and release as emotion-infused sensorimotor records, Lichtenberg observes that motor activity is the infant's first language.

Damasio (2000) even suggests that self-consciousness first appears as a nonverbal, felt "story" about the changes taking place in our bodies as we interact with each other and the environment.

We are convinced that, from infancy on, we experience the world as it is transmitted through our cultures – through stories as well. Perhaps no one has more forcefully and persuasively explicated the pervasive role of culture in narrative than Bruner. As he puts it:

> The very shape of our lives – the rough and perpetually changing draft of our autobiography that we carry in our minds – is understandable to ourselves and to others only by virtue of . . . cultural systems of interpretation.
>
> (Bruner, 1990, p. 33)

Bruner has also noted that "Without Trouble there is no narrative, no story" (2017, p. 7). We might think of trauma as exactly the sort of "trouble" that should generate narratives. In Chapter 2, we outline our understanding of trauma as embodied, and in Chapter 4 we describe the relationship between narrative and transference in the context of trauma.

Perhaps our efforts to write about the culturally informed embodied stories that fill the silences between words are doomed insofar as we must use words. Still, we feel that keeping these silences in mind makes a difference. You, our reader, must decide if this is true.

Note

1 The expression "The silence between the words" is borrowed from the Norwegian poet and psychologist, Helge Torvund (2021), who wrote "Stilla mellom orda" inspired by the Canadian-Icelandic poet Kristjana Gunnars.

References

Beebe, B., & Lachmann, F. (2014). *The origins of attachment: Infant research and adult treatment*. New York and London, England: Routledge Taylor & Francis Group.

Bruner, J. (1990). *Acts of meaning*. Cambridge, MA: Harvard University Press.

Bruner, J. (1991). The narrative construction of reality. *Critical Inquiry, 18*(1), 1–21.

Damasio, A. R. (1994/1995). *Descartes' error*. New York: Avon Books.

Damasio, A. R. (2000). *The feeling of what happens*. London: William Heinemann.

Damasio, A. R. (2010). *Self comes to mind*. London: William Heinemann.

Dillon, M. C. (1997). *Merleau-Ponty's ontology*. Evanston, IL: Northwestern University.

Frank, R., & LaBarre, F. (2010). *The first year and the rest of your life: Movement, development and psychotherapeutic change*. New York and London, England: Routledge.

Freud, S. (1890/1905/1953). Psychical (or mental) treatment. In J. Strachey (Ed. & Trans.), *The standard edition of the complete psychological works of Sigmund Freud* (Vol. 7, pp. 283–302). London, England: The Hogarth Press.

Freud, S. (1921/1955). Group psychology and the analysis of the ego. In J. Strachey (Ed. & Trans.), *The standard edition of the complete psychological works of Sigmund Freud* (Vol. 18, pp. 65–144). London, England: The Hogarth Press.

Freud, S. (1923/1961). The Ego and the Id. In J. Strachey (Ed. & Trans.), *The standard edition of the complete psychological works of Sigmund Freud* (Vol. 19, pp. 1–66). London: The Hogarth Press.

Frie, R., & Sauvayre, P. (2022). *Culture, politics and race in the making of interpersonal psychoanalysis: Breaking boundaries*. London and New York: Routledge.

Gallese, V. (2009). Mirror neurons, embodied simulation, and the neuronal basis of social identification. *Psychoanalytic Dialogues, 19*, 519–536.

Hustvedt, S. (2010). *The shaking woman or a history of my nerves*. New York: Henry Holt & Company.

Klein, G. (1976). *Psychoanalytic theory – An exploration of essentials*. New York: International Universities Press, Inc.

Lakoff, G., & Johnson, M. (1980). *Metaphores we live by*. Chicago, IL and London, England: The University of Chicago Press.

Lakoff, G., & Johnson, M. (1999). *Philosophy in the flesh*. New York: Basic books.

Lichtenberg, J. D. (2017). The dialogic nature of narrative in creativity and the psychoanalytic dialogue. In J. D, Lichtenberg, F. M. Lachmann & J. Fosshage (Eds.), *Narrative and meaning: The foundation of mind, creativity, and the psychoanalytic dialogue*. London, England and New York: Routledge.

Meltzoff, A. N., & Decety, J. (2003). What imitation tells us about social cognition: A rapprochement between developmental psychology and cognitive neuroscience. *Philosophical Transactions of the Royal Society of London B, 358*, 491–500.

Merleau-Ponty, M. (1945/1996). *Phenomenology of perception*. London, England and New York: Routledge.

Merleau-Ponty, M. (1960/1964). *Signs* (Trans. R. C. Mccleary). Evanston, IL: Northwestern University Press.

Nebbiosi, G., & Federici, S. (2008). We got rythms. In F. S. Anderson (Ed.), *Bodies in treatment. The unspoken dimension* (pp. 213–233). New York, NY: The Analytic Press.

Nebbiosi, G., & Federici, S. (2022). Miming and clinical psychoanalysis: Enhancing our intersubjective sensibility. *Psychoanalytic Inquiry, 42*(4), 266–277.

Reich, W. (1933/1949/1972). *Character analysis.* New York: Farrar, Straus and Giroux.

Schafer, R. (1976). *A new language for psychoanalysis.* New Haven, CT and London, England: Yale University Press.

Sletvold J., Training Analysts to Work With Unconscious Embodied Expressions: Theoretical Underpinnings and Practical Guidelines, 2012, *Psychoanalytic Dialogues* 22(4):410–429

Sletvold, J. (2014). *The embodied analyst – From freud and reich to relationality.* London, England and New York: Routledge Taylor & Francis Group.

Smith, Z. (2021). Fascinated to presume. In defense of fiction. *The New York Review of Books.* Retrieved from www.nybooks.com/articles/2019/10/24/zadie-smith-in-defense-of-fiction/

Spinoza, B. (1982). *The ethics.* Indianapolis, IN: Hackett Publishing Co., Inc. (First published 1677)

Torvund, H. (2021). Stilla Mellom Orda – Livet me lever går stort sett føre seg i det språklause. *Klassekampen,* 11 May.

Venuti, L. (2000). *The translation studies reader* (Ed., Lawrence Venuti and Mona Baker). London, England and New York: Routledge.

Chapter 2

Foreign bodies

From interpretation to translation

Try as we may to bring our language as close as possible to our own and our patients' lived experience, and much as we are able to gain some sense of what another person is feeling through automatic and deliberate imitation, we believe that it is impossible to precisely capture and describe what is experienced. For one thing, as Jon has observed (Sletvold, 2014), we filter our experience of others through our own subjectivities. Moreover, we cannot even know ourselves well enough to be completely aware of what is being filtered in our perceptions of the other person.

In light of this humbling awareness, we have come to believe that something like a translational process may be necessary. However, what we have in mind differs greatly from the traditional form of translation in psychoanalysis – interpretation. Interpretation, as originally conceived by Freud, involves the analyst's translation of the patient's unconscious wishes and fantasies into conscious verbal formulations. The form of translation we have come to believe is needed involves communication between the analyst's and the patient's embodied – conscious and unconscious – experiences.

To explain how we envision such a translational process, we turn to the work of Bresnahan (2021) on recent developments in the field of translation theory. Bresnahan notes that "to read for translation is to search for the interplay between the familiar and the unfamiliar, the way in which similarity and difference bleed together." Since the interplay between the familiar and the unfamiliar, similarity and difference organizes every embodied analytic encounter, we are always engaged in "reading for translation." However, what we read are not only words but our own and our patient's bodily communications.

Several of the leading translation theorists (e.g., Benjamin, 1968; Berman,1985; and Venuti, 2000) share a view of translation in literary practice as "encounters with foreignness." We would suggest that much is gained from viewing our analytic exchanges as meetings between foreign bodies.

Even when analyst and patient are of the same race, sex and ethnic background, each has developed a unique repertoire of embodied movements, gestures, ways of speaking, etc., that derives from their own differing life

DOI: 10.4324/9781003265047-3

experiences – especially those that are traumatic – and those of their parents and grandparents. While, as Kohut (1984) has pointed out, it is easier to empathize with others who are like oneself, the desire to find sameness in others may interfere with one's perceiving just how others are uniquely themselves. On the other hand, we must be aware of a tendency to exaggerate the differences between ourselves and those Zadie Smith (2021) calls "the other we are not." She (Smith, 2021) suggests that our social and personal lives always involve fictionalizations of the other-we-are-not and that we attempt to "speak" for them and through them – despite the fact that the accuracy of these attempts is never guaranteed.

Perhaps the narratives we create in our efforts to understand our patients – even to the extent that we make maximum use of our embodied ways of knowing ourselves and our patients – are always fictions filtered through our own cultures.

In treating patients from another culture, it may be somewhat easier to recognize the translational process that is almost continually at work. Being of a different race, class, sex or age from that of a patient forces us to confront our foreignness. Yet, we have come to believe that there are cultural differences, however slight, in every relationship, and that they always require translation. Differences in our cultural inheritance from past generations, as well as the impact of cultures we are exposed to, result in subtly different ways in which we communicate with our bodies.

Consider for example the ways in which we, as analysts, have learned to hold our bodies, modulate our voices and show expressions on our faces. The analytic culture transmitted by our own analysts, teachers and supervisors have not only given us a culture-specific verbal language, but an embodied one as well. And even when our patients are analysts themselves, they are affected by the verbal and bodily language that is specific to the analytic patient.

Another aspect of foreignness involves the indisputable fact that human bodies differ with respect to their sizes, shapes, odors, colors, signs of physical illness, and perceived beauty and ugliness. Yet analysts may feel estranged from their bodily responses to these differences in their patients – especially, but not always, when their sexual feelings are aroused. To the extent that they become aware of responses such as envy, attraction, repulsion, disgust and so on, analysts may experience their own bodies as foreign. They may feel a need to disavow their wish for closeness or distance from patients based on physicality as inappropriate, "un-analytic," even unethical.

But even if we acknowledge that our analytic meetings are always encounters between foreign bodies – including our own sense of foreignness regarding our own bodies – how might a translational process work? At times, differences in culture between analysts and patients seem to resemble the translational process that Bhabha (1994) refers to with respect to the postcolonial migrant. When analysts and patients engage in a power struggle to determine whose cultural language will prevail, the therapeutic relationship is likely to suffer. However, when the need for cultural translation allows for the emergence of a shared flow *of I-you-we-world* or what Bresnahan (2021) describes as the bridging of difference between people, and a "hybridity that transcends binary thinking," mutual healing becomes much more likely.

Still, the ability to tolerate the uncertainty we often experience when we confront our own or the other's body as foreign is not easily achieved. Perhaps what is needed is Pedwell's (2014) understanding of affective translation as a form of empathy. Pedwell writes:

> Affective translation . . . requires surrendering oneself to being affected by that which is experienced as "foreign." It involves multiple and ongoing processes of linguistic, cultural, temporal and affective, attunement and blurring which far from striving to achieve direct emotional equivalence . . . are engaged in the production of new affective languages, rhythms and relations.
>
> (Pedwell, 2014, p. 38)

We can think of no better way to understand empathic connectedness than the way Pedwell describes affective translation. Bresnahan (2021) notes that the roots of the word "translation," derive from the Latin "*translatio*" or carrying across. Perhaps what we need to carry us across the void separating our bodies, is belief in this complex notion of empathy as leading to new "languages, rhythms and relations," or what Donnel Stern (2019) has termed "new perceptions." As Bresnahan (2021) astutely observes, "In a very literal sense, translation can be viewed as a form of relationality." We would say that translation is a relational mode that allows for the emergence of new modes of embodied connectedness that underlie mutual healing.

We now present two clinical examples that hopefully illustrate the importance of viewing the analytic encounter as meetings between foreign bodies.

Doris and Amy

It was only in the session when my patient, Amy and I (Doris) first switched to online sessions that I became aware of our foreignness to one another. We are both white, middle-class women, well past 50 years of age, who have had many similar difficulties in life. Since our initial sessions were focused on Amy's pressing problems with her teenage son and on her ongoing divorce negotiations, we had not explored our relationship in any depth.

When Amy had appeared in my office for our in-person sessions, I could not help but notice how her stylish clothes and skillfully applied makeup enhanced her striking good looks. Since I am also careful about how I dress and always wear makeup, I had assumed that we had both been subjected to similar cultural and familial pressures. I now present some moments in a session using the approach to clinical description we outlined in Chapter 1 that revealed our foreignness to one another.

The *I* position

As I (Doris) look at Amy on the screen for the first time after the pandemic necessitated our switching to online sessions, I become aware that my smile feels forced and exaggerated. The relaxed feeling I have had throughout my body in sessions with Amy has disappeared. I cannot find a comfortable way to sit. Something is different between us but I cannot put my finger on what has changed. Then I become aware that Amy has taken pains with the lighting and background for the camera on her computer and that she has applied more make-up than usual.

The *you* position

I (Amy) turn my face to the side that makes me look more attractive in photos. I must look my best for Doris. I worry that my makeup will not disguise the asymmetry of my features. I wonder if she still likes me and wants to help me.

The *we* position

Doris and Amy suddenly feel like strangers meeting for the first time, although they have met twice weekly for six months. They are both uncomfortable and tense. The flow of dialogue between them becomes ragged and awkward silences develop.

It was only after Amy and I stared at each other in silence for a few minutes that I realized what had changed between us. Since I had not considered making myself more attractive for the computer camera, Amy suddenly seemed less known, less familiar to me.

When I commented on how successful her efforts to look beautiful had been, Amy was startled. She said that she was so used to trying to look beautiful to everyone she encountered, she had not been fully aware of all she had done to look more attractive to me. Then she tearfully acknowledged that she had worried that even the heavy makeup she applied would not hide the flaws in her beauty – flaws that the camera would expose. Our continuing explorations revealed her conviction that her perceived beauty determined the degree and quality of the attention she could expect to receive from others.

It soon became obvious that our similarities with respect to our appearance paled in comparison to our differences. While we had both had beautiful mothers who required us to echo their perfection, our mothers were hardly alike. My mother did not mercilessly berate me when she found flaws in my body in the way that Amy's mother did. Nor did she shame me in front of others for my imperfections or regulate the portions of food she served me to keep me thin. Amy felt she had no choice but to submit to her mother's pressure to become a fashion model in her teen years, despite feeling dread, verging on panic, at having her body scrutinized by strangers. Her tear-filled descriptions of her experiences during this period in which she even appeared on the cover of a fashion magazine suggested that she had been profoundly dissociated.

With the deepening of our relationship, Amy has increasingly allowed herself to experience painful feelings associated with the ways in which the disproportionate emphasis placed on her appearance has interfered with her ability to develop her considerable intelligence, creativity and capacity for caring. She has also come to understand the reasons for her compliance with her husband's wish for a "trophy wife" as well as her growing resentment at his failure to recognize her other qualities. Recognizing her role in their marital conflicts has allowed her to create a dialogue with him that appears to be leading to a more amicable ending of their marriage.

An unexpected development in our relationship has involved Amy's growing awareness that although she had devoted herself to fulfilling her mother's requirements, her intense concern about her appearance had resulted in her becoming extremely *I*-centered. As she became less certain that her only means of assuring connections with others depended on her beauty, she seemed to become more empathic to the needs of her son and others in her world. We would say there is more fluidity in her *I-you-we world* flow.

In response to Amy's recent questions about my life, I let her know that I had initially misjudged the similarity of our developmental trajectories. She admitted to having had a fantasy that our mothers were alike and that our sameness allowed me to understand her suffering. I believe that my body spoke to hers about the similarities in our relationships with our mothers. It may also have spoken to her about the differences in our cultural backgrounds that required translation. My way of speaking and moving, the legacy of my background as a native New Yorker with Jewish European grandparents, revealed subtle meanings that Amy, whose parents, grandparents and great grandparents had lived in the mid-west of the United States, could not easily grasp. Nor could I understand aspects of her embodiment that others who shared her heritage might easily "read." I hope that our meetings as foreign bodies will help us develop a translational process that will deepen our **we**-connectedness, so necessary for our healing process.

Jon and Maya

On meeting Maya, I was struck by her foreignness. She is a young woman (still in her 20s), I am an aging man (in my 70s); she is a dark-skinned African, I am a light-skinned Norwegian; she is a lesbian, I am heterosexual.

Maya sought therapy with me to help her overcome the difficulties she had with authority figures that had led to her being fired from a number of jobs.

Although she alluded to familial traumas suffered in childhood that she had never been able to tell anyone about, she indicated a wish for me to help her with here-and-now problems in living that would not necessitate her revisiting her painful past.

I now present a transformative moment in our work.

The *I* position

I (Jon) suddenly become aware that my perception of Maya, as so different from me as to almost seem like a creature from another planet, had not allowed me to echo her facial expressions, gestures, tones of voice and movements. With this realization, I relax and can let myself move in sync with her. As I notice a change in her perception of me, I become increasingly able to respond to whispered subtleties of her bodily movements. I sense that she is ready to tell me her story.

The *you* position

I (Maya) feel that Jon has suddenly changed. He is no longer regarding me as an object of curiosity to be examined. We now live in the same world. I can let him see me, know me. I can tell him about the awful experiences I had as a child.

The *we* position

There is a dramatic change in how Jon and Maya fit together. As Jon let go of his perception of Maya as someone totally different from him, his body no longer resisted the rhythms that Maya sets for him. Maya no longer needs to hold back the story of her painful past.

With each passing session, Maya added more details to a childhood filled with wrenching disruptions, sexual abuse and emotional neglect. Kidnapped by her father at age five after her mother had fled with her to a neighboring city, Maya was so grief-stricken and withdrawn, she could not go to school or play outdoors with children. But, reunited with her mother at age seven, Maya's mother became convinced that Maya had rejoined her only because she had been too difficult for her father to manage. She would leave Maya alone for long periods while she worked, and berated her mercilessly for not perfectly obeying her every command. While her mother was at work, she had been sexually assaulted by a teenage boy who lived close by. Her mother had blamed Maya, insisting that she had acted seductively.

Maya's relief at being able to tell Jon these harrowing accounts, and his ability to listen in ways that made her stories less shameful than she had imagined, seems to have increased her ability to trust others. She has established a close romantic connection with a woman who had been a friend, and she is better able to find words to let her employer know when she is unhappy at work rather than to stay home or work in a perfunctory manner.

It was only after Jon's sense of Maya as the "other he is not" diminished that he was able to allow their bodies to speak the same language. Although he still is aware of her foreignness, he no longer regards her as an alien being whose humanness is somehow diminished.

We hope these stories help to convey our understanding that a translational process involving our perception of bodies as foreign means recognizing both our sameness and difference from our patients – without exaggerating either. We believe that to the extent to which we are successful in doing so, we are able to perceive ourselves more clearly as well.

References

Benjamin, W. (1968). The task of the translator. In H. Zohn & H. Brace Jovanovich (Trans.), *Illuminations* (pp. 69–82) (Reprinted in *The Translation Studies Reader*, edited by Lawrence Venuti and Mona Baker. Routledge, 2000, pp. 15–23). New York: Routledge.

Berman, A. (1985). La Traduction comme épreuve de l'étranger. In L. Venuti (Trans.), *Translation and the trials of the foreign* (Reprinted in *The Translation Studies Reader*, edited by Lawrence Venuti and Mona Baker. Routledge, 2000, pp. 284–297). New York: Routledge.

Bhabha, H. K. (1994). How newness enters the world. In *The location of culture* (pp. 212–235). London, England and New York: Routledge.

Bresnahan, T. E. (2021). *Reading for translation: An analysis of Zadie Smith's 'white teeth' and Arundhati Roy's 'the ministry of utmost happiness* (Unpublished Thesis), University of Amsterdam, Amsterdam.

Kohut, H. (1984). *How does analysis cure?* Chicago, IL: University of Chicago Press.

Pedwell, C. (2014). *Affective relations: The transnational politics of empathy*. London, England: Palgrave Macmillan.

Sletvold, J. (2014). *The embodied analyst – From Freud and reich to relationality*. London, England and New York: Routledge Taylor & Francis Group.

Smith, Z. (2021). Fascinated to presume: In defense of fiction. *The New York Review of Books*. Retrieved from www.nybooks.com/articles/2019/10/24/zadie-smith-in-defense-of-fiction/. Accessed 27 Feb. 2021.

Stern, D. B. (2019). *The infinity of the unsaid: Unformulated experience, language, and the nonverbal*. London, England and New York: Routledge.

Venuti, L. (2000). The Translation Studies Reader. In L. Venuti & M. Baker. London and New York: Routledge.

Chapter 3

Traumatized bodies

What do bodies "say" when they talk to one another? We believe that they always communicate about *I, you, we* and *world* – and, as we tried to demonstrate in Chapter 1, this complex embodied dialogue organizes the analytic encounter. But when analysts and patients meet, their bodies very often talk about the traumatic experiences that have deeply troubled their lives.

We realize that many writers have suggested that traumatic experiences are embodied. We think, for example, of the work of Bessel van der Kolk (2014) and Peter Levine (1997, 2008). However, what we believe distinguishes our perspective on traumatic experience as embodied is that we write as psychoanalysts. We find that much psychoanalytic writing on traumatic experience either downplays or completely overlooks embodiment, or bases it on non-psychoanalytic understandings such as post-traumatic stress disorder (PTSD).

In this chapter we develop the idea that traumatizing experiences involve massive disruptions to the flow of *I, you, we* and *world*. We begin by challenging some of the prevailing ideas about the concept of trauma. For example, a commonly held assumption – despite much that has been written to the contrary (e.g., Brothers, 2014) – is that one can identify periods of time before, during and after trauma. This idea is probably most clearly exemplified by the PTSD model. The very words, "post-traumatic stress," presuppose a time after the traumatic event but it also implicitly suggests a time before trauma as well. Since, as we explain shortly, most of us are affected by responses to traumas that occurred in previous generations, and that such responses influence our experience of a recent trauma, it is impossible to identify what constitutes the "before" of trauma. We also believe that there can be no "after" trauma insofar as we remain vulnerable to embodied memories of trauma throughout our lives.

Another difficulty with the PTSD model is that the experience of trauma is often confusingly seen as having been caused by events that many people might assume would be traumatizing such as combat or rape or natural disasters. As far back as 1988, Ulman and Brothers argued that trauma does not reside in an event alone but in the meaning of that event for a specific individual. In other words, two people might undergo the same

DOI: 10.4324/9781003265047-4

experience at the same time, and only one of them might experience the event as traumatizing.

Widespread as the acceptance of this understanding has come to be, the PTSD model is still often used as the paradigm for all traumatic experience. It seems to us that the prevalence of the PTSD model has made it necessary for many contemporary clinicians to add adjectives such as "developmental," "relational," "complex," "cumulative," "insidious," "attachment" and "intergenerational" to their references to trauma, since the PTSD model does not take these phenomena into account. We suggest that emotional traumas are, by their very nature, and to varying degrees, developmental, relational, complex, cumulative, insidious and intergenerational. What makes this so will hopefully become clear after we have developed our understanding of traumatic experience.

As we noted in Chapter 1, the flow *of I, you, we* and *world* is rarely completely fluid and effortless, because humans have always lived in a traumatized and traumatizing world. We also mentioned that the *I-you-we-world* flow is, to varying degrees, difficult to attain for individuals who have such constitutional conditions as autism, ADHD, etc. We do not mean to suggest that such individuals cannot benefit from psychoanalytic treatment. Nor do we believe that these people are immune to trauma. Rather, we have found that traumatic experiences often combine with these conditions in ways that are impossible to separate.

In the face of strong emotional challenges and the revival of past traumas – either on conscious or unconscious levels of awareness – the always imperfect interweaving flow of *I, you, we* and *world* tends to slow or even freeze. At such times, the ability to perceive the interactions among self, others and the world deteriorates, and the sense of embodied wholeness is fractured. The slowing or freezing of the *I-you-we-world* flow is evident in the ritualistic preoccupations of certain patients who suffer from obsessional disorders. Peter Maduro (personal communication, September 4th, 2022) notes that they may be "wrestling with their sadness in a developmental background of insufficient holding/selfobject provision" or, as we would put it, the absence of embodied *we*-connectedness.

In our view, this deceleration occurs because the intermingling *I-you-we-world* flow is extremely complex, and complexity tends to increase experiences of uncertainty. We believe that traumatic experiences confront us with the uncertainty of our going on being whole, intact, unique individuals. They do so by destroying our belief that others will remain available for the body-to-body connectedness that underlies selfhood. Overcome by a sense of annihilating terror and helplessness, traumatized individuals immediately undertake strenuous efforts, often unconscious, to restore a sense of certainty that psychological survival is possible (Brothers, 2008).

We believe that many other analytic writers have noticed the deceleration of the I-you-we-world flow in the context of the disorders in living for which their patients sought psychoanalysis. As we see it, trauma-generated distur-bances in the flow of *I, you, we* and **world** affect many aspects of patients' lives, and manifests in a great many ways. For example, Freud, having theo-rized about the oral, anal and phallic phases of development, noticed that many of his patients became fixated at one of the phases to the detriment of the others. We suggest that these fixations accompany the slowing of *the I-you-we-world* flow. Other examples of this slowed flow are to be found in Heinz Kohut's (1971, 1977) descriptions of developmental arrests.

We believe that a great many of the restorative efforts undertaken to reduce complexity underlie much of what has come to be termed "dissocia-tion" (we recognize that dissociation, often in benign forms, is pervasive in human experiencing and we do not intend our explanation to account for its many manifestations). Our clinical experience has led us to believe that many actions taken in the aftermath of traumas that are dissociative in nature are those that involve an unrelenting focus on some aspects of experiencing to the detriment of the others. As we mentioned previously, doing so tends to reduce the experienced complexity of relational life. We have found that a preoccupation with oneself (*I*) or the other (*you*) often comes to dominate a person's experience. In these circumstances, a sense of connectedness – the sense of *we* – is weakened and, in some instances, lost.

However, there are certain forms of *we*-connectedness that also reflect dis-sociative activity. Sometimes the sense of *we* is strengthened in the absence of a fluid sensing of *I* and *you*. In Chapter 6, we explain that the *we* of fascist experience is usually a *we* without a *you*. This sort of *we* becomes the *us* of the *us-them* binary.

The emergence of *I*-centeredness, *you*-centeredness or *we*-centeredness is hardly random. A confluence of factors – most of them unconscious – are at play. A great deal is influenced by the surround; different cultures value par-ticular experiential modes over others. For example, sociologists and anthro-pologists have found that American people tend to value individuality in contrast to Japanese people who tend to value "collectiveness." Consequently, it is likely that fewer Japanese people than Americans will be perceived as *I*-centered. Modelling by caregivers, often a reflection of such cultural values, may be transmitted through the generations.

But perhaps what is most likely to affect the emergence of an emphasis on one component of the *I-you-we-world* flow is the specific nature of the trau-matic experience that is undergone. Many writers have described the emer-gence of these modes, although they may not have identified them as the result of traumatic experience. Heinz Kohut's (1971, 1977, 1984) investiga-tions into the severe narcissistic vulnerability of some grandiose individuals reveal how failures by caregivers to provide mirroring self-object experiences result in the focus on one's own needs and desires that we call *I*-centeredness.

Constitutional factors often play a role in the development of *I*-centeredness. While people suffering from painful diseases and what we call "subtle neurological conditions," such as attention deficit hyperactivity disorder (ADHD), or high-functioning autism (see Chapter 5), may not at all resemble those described as grandiose or narcissistic, their conditions may force them to focus less on others than on themselves. They may also feel so different from others in their surround as to have impoverished senses of *we*-connectedness.

The traumatic origins of *you*-centeredness are well illustrated by Bernard Brandchaft's (2007) clinical examples of "pathologically accommodating" individuals. Brandchaft stresses that pathological accommodations represent attempts to preserve needed attachments that have been traumatically threatened. He observes that these accommodations often involve the adoption of views and feelings of needed others at the expense of one's own.

We address the ways in which societal traumas tend to lead to the emergence of extreme forms of *we*-centeredness in Chapter 7.

Another dissociative measure often undertaken to reduce complexity and unbearable uncertainty in the context of trauma is the tendency to divide the perceived world into binaries. The simplification that results from the creation of such binaries as good-bad, healthy-sick, masculine-feminine, etc., may do great violence to our sense of *we*-ness (see Chapter 6). Binaries also limit the ways in which *I, you* and *we* flow in relation to **world**. When our experience of **world** is constricted by means of dichotomization, our perception of ourselves and others may be compromised as well. Captive to the constraints of binary categories, the rich complexity of our experience of *I, you, we and world* is diminished.

We recognize that dissociative activity undertaken to simplify lived experience takes a great many forms and that we have only called attention to the most common ones.

When traumatic experiences occur repeatedly in early life, often because of gross disturbances in the body-to-body relating of caregivers and children, the resulting *I*-centeredness, *you*-centeredness or *we*-centeredness, as well as the tendency to divide experience into binary categories, is frequently manifested in relational patterns that endure throughout the lifespan. In their attempts to describe this phenomenon, psychoanalysts have used such terms as "character," "character neurosis" and "neurotic styles."

These enduring styles are thoroughly embodied and greatly affect one's relationships. Doris now recalls the ways in which the bodies of an *I*-centered, *you*-centered and **we**-centered patient revealed the effect of their dissociative reactions and the ways in which they affected her bodily reactions.

The first thing I (Doris) noticed about Adam, a very successful businessman, when he entered my office for his initial session with me was the loudness of his voice. I worried that even the white noise machine in my waiting room would not muffle his verbalizations. But it was not only the volume of his voice that was striking, it was also that he seemed to be addressing a large audience of people whom he needed to enlighten. His every statement was spoken in a confident, emphatic way that invited no questions or disagreements. At times I remember feeling silenced, and when I did speak my own voice sounded unusually quiet and tentative to my ears.

Although Adam was of average height and weight, he seemed to take up a great deal of space. His large gestures and movements appeared to convey his importance and entitlement to attention from me and the outside world. I felt that I had somehow been shrunk in size and distinctness in his presence.

When Adam spoke in an arrogant dismissive way about others in his world, I would fight an urge to close my eyes, perhaps in the hope of shutting out memories of people in my past who had spoken in similar ways to me.

It was only in a session in which Adam revealed how neglected he had been by his self-involved parents, and how lonely his childhood had been, that I felt the tension in my body relax. The compassion I felt for him must have shown in my face and body, as Adam softened his voice and spoke directly to me for the first time.

In striking contrast to Adam, Lori's body seemed to communicate her extreme *you*-centeredness. Speaking in a barely audible mumbling way, she seemed to shrink herself into a corner of her chair. I imagined that Lori's lack of eye contact was a way for her to avoid calling attention to herself. Although quite attractive and slender, she dressed in nondescript, ill-fitting clothing. When she addressed me, her voice seemed full of reverence, approaching awe. Her manner seemed to say, "Please forgive me for taking up your time." In response, I felt that Lori had erected a barrier that would be challenging to reach across.

After sessions with Lori, my face would feel stiff from the exaggerated way I smiled at her. It was only after realizing that the harder I tried to encourage her to connect with me, the more she withdrew, that I leaned back and waited for her to speak. Although the silences at the beginning of our sessions felt awkward for some time, Lori soon began to fill the space I provided for her with remarkably perceptive accounts of her relational experiences.

It was not long after that she began to sit forward in her seat and to raise the volume of her voice. Her body increasingly seemed to say, "I am here. Please notice me."

A patient who exemplified an extreme form of *we*-centeredness is Diana, whose striking communication style I described in a 2012 article. Diana began a session by stating:

> Oh, you think I should go back to school. No, maybe not yet? But at some point, right? That's what I was thinking. I should go back to school, but not right now. So we both want me to go back to school, but we think I should wait a while. Why do we think I should wait? We think I need more time to be sure that I'd be happy studying massage therapy, right? I know that you enjoy being a therapist and helping people and

I like to help people a lot. Doris, maybe you think I should apply in the fall. I was also thinking maybe I should apply in the fall.

(Brothers, 2012, p. 397)

As she spoke these words, Diana perfectly imitated my bodily movements, my way of speaking and my customary gestures. To say that I found this exact mirroring disconcerting is an understatement. I felt hopeless about being able to grasp any sense of Diana's own personhood (*you*) and, as a result, my sense of myself (*I*) lacked clarity.

I was greatly relieved when Diana revealed that her severely traumatized mother had demanded flawless mirroring and that both she and her mother had been incestuously abused. Understanding the reasons for Diana's extreme **we**-centeredness eventually enabled me to stay in closer bodily alignment with her as Diana's communications – both verbal and nonverbal – became more her own.

Early and adult-onset traumatic experiences

We have the idea that when traumatic experiences occur in early life, they are likely to interfere with the *development* of a sense of embodied wholeness. That is, such individuals never experience the flow **of** *I, you, we* and **world** in a way that could be described as fluid.

What Boulanger (2009) terms "adult-onset traumas" are those that occur after some sense of embodied wholeness has developed. They are likely to be associated with the familiar PTSD symptoms such as re-experiencing, derealization and depersonalization, and are likely to involve disruptions in one's relationship to the world. We believe that many of these experiences involve intensifications of imagination and fantasy – sometimes reaching paranoidal levels – that represent efforts to compensate for the traumatic fracturing of embodied wholeness. Since adult-onset traumas often revive memories of earlier traumas and development is never completed, there can be no sharp dividing line between the two kinds of traumas. Remarkably, as Adrienne Harris (2020) has demonstrated, Sándor Ferenczi argued that both early and late-onset traumas affect somatic states.

We now offer a clinical example that illustrates the intermingling of early and adult-onset traumatic experiences.

Jon and Peter

Peter entered treatment with me (Jon) complaining that he felt quite depressed. And indeed, his appearance confirmed his self-diagnosis. His shoulders were hunched, his chest appeared sunken, and his expression was solemn. He rarely smiled or attempted light-hearted banter.

In our initial sessions Peter suggested that his depression, in some way, stemmed from the fact that, in his childhood, his father was given to frightening outbursts of anger. He also attributed his depressed mood to his troubled marriage.

From the start, our being together felt effortless, and I enjoyed our sessions. Peter clearly seemed to trust and respect me. I soon discovered that Peter had developed what we have come to describe as a "*you*-centered" relational style. In conflicts with his wife, for example, he invariably saw the situation from her perspective, at the expense of his own. We came to understand his *you*-centeredness as arising out of his attempts to deal with his father's anger. While still a young boy, he had become adept at "reading" his father's facial and bodily expressions in order to avert what might otherwise become frightening aggressive outbursts.

While I was aware that he also put my needs very much into the foreground, this had not emerged as problematic in our relationship. Having myself developed a somewhat similar *you*-centered style, I was sensitive to the many ways in which he neglected his own needs and desires. Building on this understanding, our work focused on enhancing Peter's ability to become aware of his one-sided adaptation to other's needs. As this process developed, Peter's depressive mood gradually lifted, and he was again able to devote himself to his professional activities, which included teaching. Significantly, he divorced his wife.

Our relationship seemed to have produced so many positive changes in Peter's life that I became curious about his wish to continue analysis with me. The moment I have chosen to illustrate with our embodied approach to clinical description provides the answer to my unverbalized question.

The *I* position

I (Jon) see Peter on the screen, seated in an intensely focused way as he stares directly into my eyes. I am filled with a sense of anticipation wondering if Peter will finally signal that our work together is coming to an end. I feel alert, engaged and delighted to be involved in this rich analytic process.

The *you* position

I (Peter) am very excited to tell Jon about the new memories that have suddenly flooded me. I have begun to remember terrible experiences with my ex-wife that I had forgotten until now. I have been traumatized as much by them as by my experiences with my father. Somehow I know that Jon is eager to hear about them. I have no wish to hold any of these memories back even though they have been very frightening. I tell him about the time my wife came at me with a knife, and I feared she would kill me. I have never felt so energized and in touch with my own bodily sensations.

The we position

Jon and Peter are moving in synchrony. They are unconsciously echoing one another's movements and facial expressions. They are like dancers who have so carefully learned the steps, there can be no doubt that the outcome will result in a good performance. Jon is receiving the surprising memories as if Peter had given him a precious gift.

Following this session, I realized that Peter's memories of traumatic experiences in his marriage came just after Doris and I had begun to focus on differences between traumatic experiences in early life and adult-onset traumas. Had he become so attuned to me that he detected subtle differences in the ways I listened to his descriptions of early traumatic experiences, as compared with events that occurred more recently? It is hard for me to answer with any degree of certainty.

As more memories emerged about his terrifying experiences with his wife, Peter was struck by their difference from his traumatic experiences in childhood. While he felt some degree of competence and control in dealing with his father, his memories as an adult filled him with intense anxiety and helplessness, especially when he recalled how difficult it had been to predict when a verbal or physical attack from his wife would overwhelm him.

To my surprise, Peter went on to recover fresh traumatic memories from his childhood, particularly some involving interactions with his mother. In contrast to vivid memories of his father, Peter's memories of his mother had been quite vague, but he had presented an overall image of a caring mother. His fresh memories painted a different picture. For example, he remembered that when he was five years old, he had delighted in applying colorful paint to his penis. He now remembered how controlling she had been and how fiercely she demanded obedient behavior. He also remembered having developed strategies to avoid her controlling eyes.

My input during the emergence of his new memories, which lasted over several months, were mostly about sharing images and associations that appeared to me while listening. My comments turned out to be very productive insofar as they often led him to recall more and more traumatizing experiences that occurred in his early life.

I have become aware that the similarity of our embodied styles, which derived from our both having had to mollify anger-prone fathers, had both negative and positive repercussions for the treatment. At first, it seemed so natural for Peter to have developed his *you*-centered style in response to a raging father, that I had not realized how much of what he recalled was in line with my expectations. When I became interested in traumatic experiences in his adult life, he responded by remembering more and more horrendous experiences with his ex-wife.

I am hopeful that as we continue, Peter will also be able to express his disappointments in aspects of our interactions. This would represent a major step toward his integrating heretofore dissociated aspects of his *I* experiencing.

Imagination and embodiment

We have often noticed that patients – especially some who have undergone frequent traumatic experiences in childhood – substitute imagination and fantasy for embodied connectedness. Some have done so to such a great degree that they have lost touch with what is actually happening in their worlds such that their experience is marked by delusions and paranoid preoccupations.

It is well known that when traumatic experiences engender unbearably painful feelings, these experiences, or parts of them, may be lost to conscious awareness. When horrific traumas of this sort occur early in life, they sometimes become accessible through the development of imaginary characters or alters. Patients who use this survival strategy may be diagnosed as suffering from dissociative identity disorder.

We do not mean to suggest an either/or relationship between imagination and embodiment. In the absence of ongoing trauma, imagination and embodiment are in great harmony. Thus, for example, we need to use our imaginations to maintain embodied connectedness to others who are not close by. And, of course, we believe that dreams and fantasies – so often triumphs of creative imagination – go hand in hand with embodied wholeness.

The following clinical example involves the use of imagination in the absence of embodied connectedness.

Doris and Marcia

Marcia, an extremely intelligent, 29-year-old white woman, sought treatment in the hope of gaining relief from crippling anxiety that, at times, involved suicidal ideation. Her trauma history involved sexual abuse by a babysitter and a period of extreme neglect by both parents during their stormy divorce when she was ten years old.

Although Marcia had suffered from severe anorexia as a young teenager, by the time she entered treatment with me she was considerably overweight. I was struck by her relentless focus – usually critical – on her appearance. She expressed disappointment in the way her hair looked, how a new dress fit her, whether her skin was clear, etc. Driving herself relentlessly to meet the demands of a stressful job, she had often deprived herself of sleep and recreational activities. Her frequent self-loathing remarks often contained references to being "fat." We discovered that her gaining and losing weight reflected conflicts around her wish to comply with her mother's demands for her bodily perfection and her rebellious refusal to meet them.

A few months after we had begun to work together, Marcia asked why I wasn't urging her to take steps to remove the pounds she had gained. She was amazed when I responded that I had no intention of asking her to lose weight. She had assumed that I was invested in her regaining her slim appearance so that I could feel that I was an effective therapist. Since my mother had been very focused on my appearance, I had little trouble understanding her assumption that any caregiving she could hope to receive from a woman might involve intrusive attempts at controlling her.

Although Marcia reported feeling relieved that I was not going to instruct her about controlling her food intake, and she seemed to become less guarded in her verbalizations, what I first assumed to be a growing sense of embodied connectedness between us proved to be shallow and easily disrupted. No effortless flow of an intermingling of *I-you-we-world* had developed between us, and there was no fluid echoing and reechoing of our movements. As Marcia's anxiety intensified, I became more and more fearful that our relationship would bring her no relief.

By the end of the first year of our work together, Marcia had managed to lose a great deal of weight. We both worried that her food restrictions and prolonged periods of intense exercise indicated that she would once again become anorectic.

The moment I want to highlight came after she had made a trip home. "I can't stand feeling terrified that I'll gain weight again," she moaned. Then she confessed, "It's not enough that my mother said that I look good because I've lost so much weight." She imagined her mother saying, "You're bone thin. If you lose any more weight, you won't be here at all." Insofar as Marcia's report of these imagined words from her mother were weighted with dense meanings and were accompanied by strong feelings in both of us, I now use our approach to clinical description to describe what happened between us when she spoke them.

The I position

I (Doris) notice a feeling of tightness in my chest that I associate with being anxious. My heartbeat becomes more rapid, and I breathe deeply to calm myself. I feel that I must listen carefully lest I fail to grasp something important that Marcia is trying to convey. When she tells me that she imagines her mother saying, "You're bone thin," I'm flooded with memories of my own mother's voice commenting on my appearance and suddenly grasp the depth of Marcia's despair. When she looks at me and tears spring to her eyes, I realize that she has registered my compassion. We are meeting as if for the first time.

The you position

I (Marcia) sit in a stiff unmoving upright posture and run my tongue over my bottom lip in a way that is somewhat self-soothing. I stare fixedly straight ahead, unable to look at Doris. When I repeat the words I imagined my mother saying – "You're bone thin" – I clench my jaw and speak without a hint of emotion. When I stop speaking, I look at Doris. She is really looking at me, taking me in, and I see that she understands my suffering. Tears spring to my eyes.

The *we* position

Both Doris and Marcia feel that this exchange represents a turning point in their relationship. Marcia had silently signaled that she had something important to convey and both worried that Doris wouldn't understand its importance. When both are struck by the meanings embedded within the "bone thin" fantasy, they are connected in a new way.

What is significant about this moment is not only that it greatly deepened my relationship with Marcia, but that it also set the stage for exchanges that allowed us to better understand the "bone-thin" fantasy and what it meant for the healing process. For one thing, Marcia confirmed that her mother's seeing her as "bone thin" emerged in the absence of bodily connectedness. For Marcia, physical proximity plays an important role in her ability to feel connected to others. Despite the lack of emotional closeness we initially experienced, Marcia felt somewhat protected against her need to comply with or defy her mother during our in-person sessions. Little wonder that she objected strenuously when the COVID crisis necessitated our shifting to online sessions. Physically far from me on her visit home, her conflicted feelings reemerged.

We came to understand that the imaginary "bone-thin" response from her mother served Marcia in at least two ways: first, if she were once again as thin as an anorectic, her mother (and I) might show the care and concern Marcia received during her teenage hospitalization. And, secondly, if her mother could not possibly think that she could lose any more weight, Marcia felt immune from a repetition of her mother's (and my) contempt for her imperfect body. It was only when she felt that she finally had the attention of a woman who wanted to see her for who she was, and to deeply understand her pain, that the *we*-connectedness of healing could begin.

Summarizing the two clinical examples

Our write-ups of our work with Peter and Marcia hopefully illustrate aspects of our understanding of traumatic dissociation. For Peter, early traumatic experiences with his parents resulted in a pronounced *you*-centeredness that permeated his relationships – including his relationship with Jon. Marcia's early traumas resulted in her *I*-centered concentration on her body – especially her weight. To counter early failures in embodied connectedness as well as her physical and emotional distance from Doris during her vacations, Marcia relied on her imagined conversation with her mother.

It also is apparent that we both found similarities between our patients and ourselves. Jon's *you*-centered orientation allowed him to grasp Peter's mode of relating, and Doris's experiences with her own mother allowed her to grasp Marcia's intense preoccupation with her weight. We believe that we did not have to verbalize these similarities to our patients; they were communicated between our talking bodies. We cannot possibly register all the information that we transmit to our patients in this way, but we imagine that even more is passed along in the silences between the words.

Trauma through the generations

We do not see trauma itself as transmitted from one generation to the next. Rather, what is passed from parents to children are the efforts taken to restore a sense of embodied wholeness. Such modelling occurs in the earliest embodied interactions between infants and caregivers (Brothers, 2014). While some people simply adopt the complexity-reducing efforts that have been modeled by their parents and grandparents, other people strenuously oppose any pressure to conform to a familial pattern. So, for example, a person who learns that *you*-centeredness will allow them to maintain needed connections may instead become intensely *I*-centered. Much depends on how insular the family system is and whether others in the surround support alternative ways of being in the world. Other considerations include the pressures within the culture and the extent to which it promotes conformity or independence. Much also depends on constitution. The degree of intelligence, beauty, charm, etc., possessed by the individual largely determines how others outside the family either enforce compliance or support resistance.

Although we cannot mention all of the psychoanalysts who have shown the influence of traumas in past generations on the psychoanalytic relationship, we find the writings of Adrienne Harris and co-authors on *Demons in the Consulting Room: Echoes of Genocide, Slavery and Extreme Trauma in Psychoanalytic Practice* (Harris et al., 2017) to be powerfully on target. Their work demonstrates how traumatic experiences have effects across multiple generations, and how these effects manifest in the consulting room.

Do analysts treat trauma?

Since trauma is ever present in our world, every patient is, to some extent, a traumatized human being. So, in a sense, our therapeutic relationships always involve trauma. Yet, it is tempting to say that, from the perspective of embodiment, we do not treat trauma at all. For one thing, we have found that patients suffer less from the actual traumatic experiences they have lived through than they do from the harmful effects of the survival strategies they needed to employ. Many of the complaints for which our patients seek our help reflect the measures that they have employed to combat the effect of traumatizing helplessness and uncertainty.

For another, we believe that every traumatic experience must be seen in terms of the context of a person's constitutional inheritance and the world in which they live. This means that how bodies talk about their traumas reflects each person's physical embodiment – their relative health, illness and disability, and the sociopolitical and cultural systems in which they live. It also reflects the emotional climate in which they were raised and the extent to which their emotional needs were met. Were there supportive others in their environment who could bear witness to their struggles? Did they feel that the language their bodies spoke was understood and affirmed? How much of their traumatic experience did they need to dissociate? The answers to these questions play crucial roles in how the bodies of analyst and patient talk to one another.

References

Boulanger, G. (2009). *Wounded by reality – Understanding and treating adult-onset trauma.* New York and London, England: Psychology Press, Taylor & Francis Group.

Brandchaft, B. (2007). Systems of pathological accommodation and change in analysis. *Psychoanalytic Psychology, 24*(4), 667–687.

Brothers, D. (2008). *Toward a psychology of uncertainty: Trauma-centered psychoanalysis.* New York: Analytic Press.

Brothers, D. (2012). Trauma, gender and the dark side of twinship. *International Journal of Psychoanalytic Self Psychology, 7*(3), 391–403.

Brothers, D. (2014). Traumatic attachments: Intergenerational trauma, Dissociation and the analytic relationship. *International Journal of Psychoanalytic Self Psychology, 9*(1), 3–15.

Harris, A. E. (2020). Thalassa, confusion of the tongues, The unwelcome child and his death-instinct. Sándor ferenczi's unfolding model of trauma. *Attachment: New Directions in Relational Psychoanalysis and Psychotherapy, 14*, 1–22.

Harris, A., Kalb, M., & Klebanoff, S. (2017). *Demons in the consulting room: Echoes of genocide, slavery and extreme trauma in psychoanalytic practice.* London and New York: Routledge Taylor & Frances.

Kohut, H. (1971). *The analysis of the self.* New York: International Universities Press, Inc.

Kohut, H. (1977). *The restoration of the self.* New York: International Universities Press, Inc.

Kohut, H. (1984). *How does analysis cure?* (Ed. A. Goldberg & P. Stepansky). Chicago, IL: Chicago University Press.

Levine, P. (1997). *Waking the tiger: Healing trauma.* Berkeley, CA: North Atlantic Books.

Levine, P. (2008). *Healing trauma: A pioneering program of restoring the wisdom of your body.* Louisville: Sounds True.

Ulman, R. B. & Brothers, D. (1993). *The shattered self: A psychoanalytic study of trauma.* Hillsdale, NJ: Analytic Press.

Van der Kolk, B. (2014). *The body keeps the score: Brain, mind and the body in the healing of trauma.* New York: Viking.

Chapter 4

Embodying dissociation

Having briefly described our understanding of dissociation as it occurs in the context of traumatic experience in Chapters 2 and 3, we now explain how our understanding is similar to, and different from, what we call "the dissociation-enactment model." We also offer a fresh view of what has been termed, "multiple self-states." We hope that our clinical example that ends this chapter will clarify our position.

Dissociation as originally conceived of by Freud (1893/95) and Janet (1907) referred to the splitting of mental contents. For many relational theorists today, dissociated aspects of both the patient's and the analyst's experience emerge in analytic relationships in the form of what has become known as "enactments." We consider the "dissociation-enactment model" to represent a large step towards an embodied understanding of dissociation, insofar as it views dissociation as enacted bodily between therapist and patient. Donnel Stern (2019) aptly referred to this as "the interpersonalization of dissociation." Nevertheless, we quarrel with the way this model still views dissociation as a splitting of the contents of the mind.

As we see it, the dissociation-enactment model maintains a conceptual split between embodied dyadic interaction on the one hand and the internal mind on the other. Dyadic interactions are either seen as triggering the release of dissociated mental content, or dissociative mental content is understood to influence the relations between analyst and patient. (e.g., Bromberg, 2011). This split might be understood as a hangover from the dissociation theory of Freud and Janet. In this model the dissociated hidden mental content, like the repressed, needs to become consciously known and integrated with self-experience.

We suggest that what is commonly referred to as "splitting" is an emotional reaction to painful, traumatizing experiences – those that threaten psychological well-being and thereby make it impossible to maintain a nuanced perception of and reaction to what is happening. In other words, it results from the disruption of the *I-you-we-world* flow. When such experiences are revived in therapeutic exchanges, the first reaction by members of the dyad is often a sense that "something isn't quite right" (BPCSG, 2013). Although

DOI: 10.4324/9781003265047-5

analysts may later conceptualize some sort of splitting in their patients' minds, patients themselves seldom experience what is going on in terms of splitting. *Splitting, per se, is not an embodied experience.*

As far as we can tell, The Boston Change Process Study Group (BCPSG) was the first to point out limitations in the dissociation-enactment model (alternatively referred to as the dissociative self-state model). They (BCPSG, 2013) offer an understanding of dissociation and enactment that in some ways anticipated the view we hold. They write: "An alternative to the dissociative self-state model . . . emphasizes implicit memory processes in bodily comportment and style of relating with others" (BCPSG, 2013, p. 727).

Donnel Stern (2019) has taken steps in the same direction. He no longer sees the goal of analysis to be the transformation of enacted unformulated experience into verbal communication. He writes:

> The clinical observation that originally ignited my interest in dissociation and enactment . . . is that enactments are not dissolved by verbal understanding at all, but by the enactor's development of a *new, nonverbal perception* of the other.
>
> (p. 68, original italics)

According to Stern, this new perception first appears as a change in one's nonverbal grasp of what the other is like – a new nonverbal sense of the other that might be, but does not have to be, articulated verbally.

Our view aligns with that of D. B. Stern and BCPSG, insofar as our understanding of dissociation is also founded on bodily interaction rather than on mental splitting. We take the position that a disruptive experience between analysts and patients is usually the result of ongoing interactions in which embodied communication has begun to break down. In the therapeutic dyad, as in other relationships, expectations are created about what can be anticipated from the other person while the two are together. BCPSG writes:

> [O]ver time a fittedness of joint directionality develops within the dyad, partly on the basis of the two partners implicitly coordinating their directions into a shared one.
>
> (BCPSG, 2013, p. 729)

We understand the development of shared direction as involving a growing feeling of embodied connectedness that depends on the ability to keep both self (*I*) and other (*you*) in mind. With the breakdown of embodied connectedness, dialogue becomes difficult and discussions often devolve into angry exchanges or silent protests. In our view, this is most likely to happen when one or both parties unconsciously experience what is happening as repeating or resembling traumatizing life experiences. When this occurs in the analytic relationship, either the patient or the analyst (or both) is experienced as failing to meet the other's needs for empathic contact and may even be viewed as attacking and dangerous.

We avoid using the term "enactment" in our discussion of therapeutic disruptions for many reasons. Sletvold (2016) has reviewed the use of this term over time. He notes that while enactments were first viewed as discrete events – disruptions of the verbal flow – it has come to be seen as an ever-present part of the analytic process. For example, Aron and Atlas (2015) situate enactments within the larger flow of therapeutic process. We object to the way the word, "enactment," refers to a performance of past experience. From an embodied perspective, therapeutic disruptions result from the ways bodies communicate in the present moment, usually when memories of past traumas are revived.

When what have become known as enactments are considered from the vantage point of the intermingling body-based sensing **of *I, you, we*** and ***world***, attention is shifted from what supposedly is going on "inside" each participant to what is going on between them. Focus shifts from the hypothetical dissociated experience "inside" an individual, to the specific affective exchanges occurring in the moment. When a disruption occurs, usually because of the threat of some recurrence of trauma, the therapist is called upon to take some kind of "action." This may be a verbal response, a change of expression or body posture, silence or stillness.

In such situations, we analysts must rely on our embodied feelings about what is happening in order to empathically tune in to the patient's experience as well as our own. We may address the turn away from body-to-body connectedness, or we may choose not to. There is no correct way to respond.

In all therapeutic interactions, patients and analysts are continuously feeling out their relational fit by observing one another's expressions, gestures, movements, tones of voice, etc. These bodily events are not caused by pre-existing mental states. Mind becomes inseparable from "the *way* in which a living body acts, not something separable from, hidden behind, or leading to its action" (BCPSG, 2013, p. 740). From this perspective, change is not limited to verbal or cognitive integration in one person, but is conceived as an interactive integration occurring in the dyad.

In addition, perceptions of one another are not divided into the verbal and nonverbal. By integrating all aspects of experiences of *I* and *you*, embodied wholeness emerges (which is based on a sense of *we*). In the words of BCPSG, "The relational meaning adheres in the whole of how the threads of imagery, words, and affect come together in a relational exchange" (2013, p. 742).

We also recognize that what is happening in the world plays a decisive role in the revival of earlier traumatic experiences of patients and therapists. When both analyst and patient are profoundly affected by existential threats, such as those posed by the climate crisis, the COVID pandemic and political strife, disruptions to the *I-you-we-world* flow become much more likely. Moreover, we appreciate the ways in which the cultural backgrounds of the analytic couple affect the form taken by these disruptions.

From multiple self-states to disruptions of the *I-you-we-world* flow

Philip Bromberg (2011) has been the leading proponent of the notion that human experiencing involves multiple self-states. He writes:

> Self-states are highly individualized modules of being, each configured by its own organization of cognitions, beliefs, dominant affect and mood, access to memory, skills, behaviors, values, actions, and regulatory physiology.
>
> When all has gone well developmentally, each self-state is compatible enough with the modes of being that are held by other self-states to allow overarching coherence across self-states, which in turn creates the capacity for sustaining the experience of internal conflict.
>
> (Bromberg, 2011, p. 73)

Bromberg notes that dissociation is a healthy, adaptive function of the mind that allows individual self-states to function optimally when full immersion in a single reality, a single strong affect and a suspension of one's self-reflective capacity is exactly what is called for or wished for. However, at times, in the throes of dissociation, "one part of the patient is attempting to secure her bond with the analyst by speaking as if her task were to obliterate another part of herself as sick and replace it with a 'healthy' part" (p. 70).

Our understanding, like Bromberg's, also links dissociative processes and the tendency to focus on only certain aspects of experiencing, both as part of healthy adaptive functioning (as, for example, when we become absorbed in a book or a film) and as a means of "going on being" in the face of traumatic experiences. However, we object to the term "self-states" insofar as it alludes to what is going on intra-psychically, even when the individual is dealing with others and the world. In our view there can be no "*self*-states", there are only *self-with-other* ways of experiencing and acting, or from our perspective, a complex, intermingling flow of *I, you, we* and *world.*

Although we have posited that under certain conditions a person may become *I*-centered, we do not believe that the experience of others – *you* or *we* – is ever completely absent, except in the most extreme forms of psychosis. When a person becomes absorbed in a book or a film, they are intensely connected with the material represented and for a short while turn their attention away from themselves and others. However, as we have pointed out, in the context of trauma, an intense focus on *I, you* or *we* is likely to characterize their experience over long periods of time (we explain how an experience of *we* based on our sameness and difference from others sometimes becomes transformed into the *us-them* binary in Chapter 6).

The most extreme forms of *I*-centeredness in clinical practice involves those patients who suffer from conditions known as dissociative identity disorder. Most patients suffering from these conditions have experienced many horrific traumas in early life. Because of the unbearably painful nature of these traumatic experiences, and the absolute rupture of embodied connectedness they entail, these patients imaginatively create what have been termed "alter" personalities who "remember" the horrific experiences without incapacitating the whole individual.

We believe that many patients who have not completely encapsulated memories of trauma in the form of alter personalities relate to their analysts with a variety of *I*-experiences. One of Doris' patients alternatively related to her as an angry, faultfinding adult, and as a young child unable to make sense of the world. What we discovered is that the angry faultfinding *I* she presented was a vivid imitation of her hostile, shaming mother. The childlike *I* seemed to implore Doris to relate to her as the little girl who urgently needed guidance, understanding and protection. These alternating *I* experiences seemed to have provided an embodied replica of her past relationship and provided opportunities for making up missed experiences in early life. Because they were so interconnected with her experiences within her therapeutic relationship, we believe it would have been misleading to conceptualize what was happening in terms of "self-states."

In summary, we suggest replacing the concept of multiple self-states with the understanding that one's sensing of oneself (*I*) may vary from context to context. The experiencing of *I*, no matter how variable, is inseparable from the experiencing of *you*, *we* and *world*. We also object to the way the term, self-state, indicates a stable, enduring way of being, rather than an experience that is context-sensitive.

To illustrate our understanding of dissociation as embodied, we now recount Jon's relationship with a woman whose dissociative symptoms had led her to be diagnosed as schizophrenic.

Jon and Laura

12 years ago, when I (Jon) began therapy with Laura, a 34-year-old Caucasian woman, I soon discovered that the biggest practical challenge I faced was how to end our sessions. Laura had already established a routine requiring that her therapists say "excuse me" several times before she could leave them. After saying "excuse me" over and over to end one session, I felt compelled to usher her out of my office when she refused to leave. She ended the therapy at this point.

I was very surprised, but also pleased when, 11 years later, Laura contacted me to ask if she could resume therapy. I took it to mean that she had kept some good memories and feelings about our previous work together.

Although Laura had been released from the outpatient unit of a hospital where she had been an inpatient for several years, she felt that she still needed therapy. She explained that six years earlier, she had been admitted to a closed psychiatric ward after hearing voices and that she had been diagnosed with schizophrenia. Laura's experience of hearing voices had been very frightening to her and she did not seem to object to the diagnosis.

Upon her return, I felt that Laura had improved considerably. I experienced her as far less rigidly demanding than she had been in the past and I felt hopeful that the emerging sense of *we* that was developing between us would become stronger over time.

Laura had suffered from both neglect and abuse throughout her childhood. Having little contact with her father, she lived with her drug-addicted mother who was often verbally and, at times, severely physically abusive. She once broke Laura's nose in a fit of rage. Several of her mother's many boyfriends abused Laura sexually.

I soon realized that many of Laura's problems in living were a consequence of her intense focus on herself (*I*) to the detriment of her empathy for others. Moreover, her extreme vulnerability to memories of being verbally assaulted in childhood led her to interpret rather benign comments by others as insults and unjust criticisms. She could not see that she had contributed to these relational disruptions.

Laura still hears very frightening voices that she is convinced come from outside herself. These auditory hallucinations have been most likely to occur during interruptions in our sessions, or when she experiences loneliness after a disappointing encounter with a friend. Such experiences often remind her of her terrifyingly lonely childhood

While Laura has begun to tolerate my comments about what happens between us, she still tends to interpret subtle changes in my voice or posture as indicating that I am angry with her. While in the past she would require apologies from me to justify her heated reactions, she is sometimes able to accept my assurances that I feel no anger toward her and to explore what has led her to assume that I was angry. I now present what occurred between us following her report that neighbors had been taunting her with sounds of lovemaking from the nearby apartment.

The "*I*" position

I (Jon) am aware of holding my breath. I feel an impulse to drum my fingers to relieve my stress and an urge to close my eyes. I dread feeling compelled to act as if I believe that her accusations about the neighbors were justified, despite my doubts. My body temperature rises and I break out in a sweat. I feel angry at Laura for putting me in this predicament and worried about how to address it without shaming her.

The "*you*" position

My (Laura's) whole body has begun to tremble and my features contract into a tight frown. I want to shout in anger to protest being treated without consideration. I cannot meet Jon's eyes.

The "*we*" position

They are both attempting to ward off their anger and they are both afraid of a repetition of past disruptions. Jon worries that Laura will soon turn her anger from her neighbors onto him. Laura dreads finding that her sense of reality will again be subject to doubt. Jon suddenly realizes that a repetition of past disruptions is not inevitable. He relaxes and feels ready to relate his feeling responses to Laura.

I was able to tell Laura that she had probably sensed that I had not accepted her understanding of what happened. I added that I believed we had both been afraid that our anger would disrupt our connectedness. Even before putting this into words my bodily response to Laura had probably informed her that I more deeply understood her experience and that I was willing to meet her in a different way. She reciprocated by opening herself to my experience and was no longer convinced that I was bent on distorting her sense of reality. She wondered if she had interpreted sounds from the neighboring apartment as deliberate efforts to torment her with their lovemaking because she had been overcome with longing for love and attention after a disappointing date. With this embodied exchange it could be said that a new sense of *we* emerged between us and that what might have become a disruptive exchange was averted.

Jon's experience with Laura hopefully illustrates our embodied understanding of dissociation. We believe that when memories of past traumas are revived in the analytic relationship, dissociative experiences are likely to arise. We understand Laura's voices as an extreme form of the replacement of embodied connectedness with imagination.

To summarize our view: what has been thought of as dissociation results from the disruption of the complex intermingling of the *I-you-we-world* flow such that some of these essential aspects of experience are emphasized at the expense of the others. We believe that by attending to the first signs of our own embodied reactions to these disruptions, as well as to those of our patients, the extreme forms of enactment that have been described in the relational literature can be moderated. As Donnel Stern (2015, 2019) suggests, the real work is already done by the time the new story falls into place.

References

Aron, L., & Atlas, G. (2015). Generative enactment: Memories from the future. *Psychoanalytic Dialogues, 25*, 309–324.

Boston Change Process Study Group. (2013). Enactment and the emergence of new relational organization. *Journal of the American Psychoanalytic Association, 61*, 727–749.

Bromberg, P. (2011). *The shadow of the tsunami and the growth of the relational mind*. London, England and New York: Routledge.

Freud, S., & Breuer, J. (1893/1895/1955). Studies on hysteria. In J. Strachey (Ed. & Trans.), *The standard edition of the complete psychological works of sigmund freud* (Vol. 2, pp. 1–251). London: The Hogarth Press.

Janet, P. (1907). *The major symptoms of hysteria*. New York: Macmillan.

Sletvold, J. (2016). The analyst's body: A relational perspective from the body. *Psychoanalytic Perspectives, 13*, 186–200. DOI: 10.1080/1551806X.2016.1156433.

Stern, D. B. (2015). *Relational freedom – Emergent properties of the interpersonal field*. London, England and New York: Routledge.

Stern, D. B. (2019). *The infinity of the unsaid: Unformulated experience, language, and the non-verbal*. London, England and New York: Routledge.

Chapter 5

Memory, narrative and the embodiment of transference

We imagine that, like us, analysts sometimes engage with patients who have forgotten part – or even the entirety – of what seems to have been a consequential traumatic experience. And, like us, they probably assume that dissociation plays a role in this forgetting (see Chapter 3).

In Chapter 2, we suggested that when the bodies of analysts and patients talk about trauma, the need to emphasize one component of the *I-you-we-world* flow as a means of simplifying experience thereby reduces a sense of uncertainty and helplessness that often arises. We now suggest that a focus on only one *I-you-we-world* component may lead to the dimming of conscious awareness of the other components. For example, those needing to focus only on themselves (we say they have become *I*-centered) may forget parts of their experience that relate to their interactions with others. Or they may selectively keep in mind aspects of their interactions with others that emphasize their own worth or importance, while forgetting aspects that fail to do so. On the other hand, patients who need to focus only on others (those we call *you*-centered), may forget aspects of their experience that remind them of their own needs and feelings.

It goes without saying that dissociative forgetting also helps patients avoid being conscious of what they fear will be the unbearable pain associated with traumatic experience. However, as we explain shortly, these seemingly "forgotten" experiences may continually influence embodied connecting.

Patients are not the only ones who forget; in the context of trauma and its revival in the therapeutic relationship, analysts are just as likely to forget painful aspects of their own experience. Their forgetting may have equally powerful effects on the embodied contact of the analytic couple. When bodies talk about the unspeakable, the analytic relationship often becomes fraught with conflict. Some relational theorists have conceptualized what happens in terms of "enactments" (see Chapter 3).

But, however frequently dissociative forgetting – either by ourselves, or our patients – affects our clinical relationships, remembering plays an equally important role. Many theorists, starting with Freud, have described the role

DOI: 10.4324/9781003265047-6

of memory, in both narrative and what has been known as transference. In this chapter we offer a view of the role of memory, both conscious and unconscious, as it relates to talking bodies in the analytic relationship, and suggest a fresh perspective on transference.

Memory in the therapeutic relationship

Freud and Breuer famously wrote: "Hysterics suffer mainly from reminiscences" (1895, p. 7). But memories, of course, are not only about traumatic suffering. They can fill us with delight, especially when they involve our connectedness to loved ones. Memory continually colors our perception of others as well as our experience of ourselves. We not only remember our past encounters with other people but also all sorts of other experiences that are evoked by what is going on in our interactions with them.

Memory, we believe, cannot be separated from imagination. As Lichtenberg notes: "Memory is no longer viewed as an accurate, stable representation of an event, but a dynamic process" (2017, p. 9). It is now widely believed that how an experience is remembered is greatly affected by the context in which it is recalled. Neuroscientists tell us that when we try to retrieve a memory, what we find is not the original memory, but the one we last recalled, and which had already been imaginatively altered. While there is much to say about remembering, what is especially important for the clinical encounter is that memories tend to be laden with feelings.

Another aspect of memory that is vitally important to our clinical relationships has to do with the form it takes. For example, we might ask if memories are always conscious. Thanks to the findings of such researchers as Schacter (1996) and Damasio (2010) we have learned that the memories that arise within the analytic encounter are both "declarative" (those that are verbal and episodic in nature) and "implicit" (those that are nonverbal and procedural in nature.) It seems likely to us that even when the verbal declarative form of memory is lost to consciousness, as is often the case for patients who focus on only one component of the *I-you-we-world* flow, implicit nonverbal memories of these events may continue to influence what happens between patients and analysts. We presume that these memories subtly affect the facial expressions of the analytic partners, how they move, gesture, speak and look at one another. We suspect that even though the changed embodiment of the analytic partners may elude verbal expression, it does not go unnoticed in the body-to-body exchange.

Freud was well aware of the ubiquity of memory and its importance in the analytic relationship. In fact, as soon as he began to develop his psychological theory, memory occupied a central place in his understanding of transference. It was in the final section of *Studies on Hysteria* that Freud first used the word "transference." He wrote: "Transference of the physician takes place through a *false connection*" (Freud & Breuer, 1893/95/1955, p. 302).

Clearly the patient's "false connection" to Freud could not have been made if she had not remembered aspects of an earlier relationship. It goes without saying that from 1895 to the present, the concept of transference has been greatly expanded and elaborated. In addition to oedipal transferences, analysts have identified positive and negative transferences, maternal and paternal transferences, erotic transferences, counter-transferences, self-object transferences and co-transferences. Yet, no matter how it is modified, we are troubled by the ways in which the concept of transference still conveys Freud's idea that transferences are experiences that reside within each individual – even when they are interacting.

Few analysts today believe that the goal of treatment is to analyze "the transference" until patients stop displacing onto analysts, and presumably others in their lives, the thoughts and feelings that arose in earlier developmental contexts. Most of us recognize that psychoanalytic healing does not depend upon fixing something inside the patient. Since memories of events and people in the pasts of both the analytic partners always shape their relationship, it follows that healing is a shared phenomenon.

Embodied narratives

Our present understanding of what has been regarded as transference, like Freud's, also involves the ways in which the therapeutic relationship depends on memory. We could not begin to develop our understanding without referring to narrative. In Chapter 1 we outlined our understanding of embodied narrative as occupying the "silence between the words" in human dialogue. Thanks to many analysts starting with Roy Schafer (1976), we also understand that the form that memories take is that of stories or narratives (see also Lichtenberg, 2017). Freud reluctantly acknowledged this in "Studies in Hysteria" when he wrote:

> It still strikes me as strange that the case histories I write should read like short stories and that, as one might say, they lack the serious stamp of science.
>
> (1893, pp. 160–161)

As we see it, both the declarative and implicit memories that flow between patients and analysts continually shape the narratives that organize the psychoanalytic encounter. Memory and feeling-drenched clinical narratives make use of the specific ways that *I, you* and **we** intermingle between analysts and patients. Moreover, the memories that influence mutually created clinical narratives are powerfully shaped by what is happening in the world in which they live as well as by experiences that formed the narratives of the analytic partner's parents and grandparents.

Transference as embodied connectedness

We have found that much of what happens between analysts and patients is too fluid and complex to be identified as any sort of specific transference. This is particularly true when memories of traumatic experiences are not being activated in the here and now of the therapeutic exchange. When, inevitably, traumatic memories are revived in the analytic relationship, the complexity of *I-you-we-world* tends to flow in slow motion, and the mutually created clinical narratives tend to become rigidified, sometimes even frozen in place. It might be said that trauma casts a spell over the clinical encounter and the analytic partners share a strange state in which stories of traumas that occurred in the distant past intermingle with those that are more recent. In the thrall cast by the activation of traumatic memories, spontaneity, playfulness and surprise may recede into the background.

We would suggest that it is just this traumatic slowing – at times even freezing – of *I-you-we-world* experiencing and the effects this has on the mutually created narratives of analysts and patients that was initially referred to as transference. In this suspended space, much that happens between the analytic partners represents attempts to ward off the re-experiencing of earlier traumas.

To illustrate our perspective on memory, narrative, transference and its intergenerational borrowings, we refer to a clinical relationship that Doris had with a young black woman we call Tracy. Doris has used this case in an earlier publication (Brothers, 2016), but we now will describe the relationship between Doris and Tracy in a way that is consistent with our embodied approach.

Doris and Tracy

In December of 2010, a severe case of Bell's palsy paralyzed half my (Doris's) face and contracted the features on the other half into a weird grimace. To say that the experience was traumatizing does not begin to capture the devastating effect my loss of facial expressivity had on my life (Brothers, 2016). I felt that I had become shamefully recognizable only as a member of a despised group of individuals – those with a disfiguring illness. Consigned to the ranks of Bell's palsy sufferers, and feeling interchangeable with all others similarly afflicted, I experienced firsthand what Levinas (1947/1987) meant by the term, "totalizing," that is, being reduced to an object to be studied, categorized or comprehended, which he contrasted with responding to the face of the other. And with that totalizing experience, my own sense of differentiated selfhood seemed to dissolve and weaken.

It was just this sense of kinship with others who feel "hostage to the shaming gaze of others" (Stolorow, 2011, pp. 107–108) that, I believe, transformed my therapeutic relationship with Tracy, a dark-skinned and stocky African American teenager. I had worked with Tracy's parents several years earlier and they had let her know that I had been helpful to them. She mentioned several times feeling impressed by the difference she perceived in her parents' relationship after they had worked with me.

Severely depressed, given to cutting the skin on her thighs and functioning well below her high capacity for academic achievement, Tracy bemoaned her difference from the thin, blond and blue-eyed girls who were popular in her prestigious New York prep school. "My parents tell me to feel proud of being Black," she once said, "but I don't." In fact, Tracy had conveyed her feeling that being darker-skinned than her younger sister and their mother was a source of unremitting shame. We had understood her cutting, in part, as her way of demonstrating her hatred of her dark skin, as well as a secret way of spiting her mother who seemed obsessed with her daughters' perfection.

I had occasionally tried to initiate a discussion with Tracy regarding the effects of racial difference on our relationship. When I asked her directly what it was like to talk about her distress over her skin color to a white woman, Tracy dismissed my concern. "I know you're trained to help people who aren't the same as you," she said. Still, I suspected that my being white was partially responsible for the emotional distance she maintained from me, and the relatively small range of feelings that she expressed in our sessions.

The session I will use to illustrate our approach to embodied clinical description and our ideas about memory, narrative and transference occurred when Tracy saw my distorted face for the first time.

The "I" position

I'm (Doris) filled with dread before Tracy arrives. My whole body feels tense and cold. I wonder if she will pull away from me out of pity or even disgust as some other patients had done. Will she feel betrayed because my physical impairment is evidence that I'm not the omnipotent, invulnerable woman she seemed to need? When she breaks into tears at her first sight of me, I'm immediately flooded with relief. As she throws her arms around me in a consoling embrace, I'm overwhelmed with tenderness for her.

The "you" position

Doris warned me (Tracy) that she's suffering from Bell's palsy and that her face is very distorted, but I had not expected to see her so horribly changed. I'm surprised by the tears that stream from my eyes and I cannot resist the urge to hold her in my arms. We are connecting in a new way. I am frightened and excited.

The "we" position

A wall between them has dissolved. Neither said a word as Tracy threw her arms around Doris, but her silent message seemed unmistakable: "Now that we're in the same boat, I can feel for you and with you." Doris's silent message to Tracy was: "Much as I hate what has happened to me, I'm glad that my visible trauma has allowed you to show me who you are." Their interwoven narrative could now be expressed as: "Being similarly afflicted, our lives and hearts are now joined and we can begin the shared venture of healing."

Needless to say, this sense of our fittedness to one another transformed our relationship. Tracy's sense of kinship with me seemed to embolden her to confront the most painful aspects of her difference from others in a deeply emotional way. But the healing this engendered was not only Tracy's. After discovering that neither my literal nor my metaphorical losses of face had estranged us – indeed it had brought us closer together – I too felt more whole.

I believe that the trauma-generated narrative shared by Tracy and me, before my Bell's palsy, gave rise to the idealizing transference that developed between us. She seems to have used the narrative of my healing powers as a therapist to allow a connection with me while avoiding the pain she felt about being black in contrast to my whiteness. She later admitted to believing that my privilege as a white woman provided me with immunity from societal hatred – an immunity she could never even hope for. My narrative involving her need to experience me as idealizable was a hedge against my own unconscious sense of vulnerability to societal hatred. Perhaps something in our way of bodily relating to one another revealed the commonalities in our histories. Violent pogroms had forced my Jewish immigrant grandparents to leave Europe for America. Tracy's African great-great-grandparents had been forced to leave their homelands as slaves. No one in either my family or Tracy's had ever spoken of these traumatic experiences, but I have little doubt that they were transmitted from body to body and from generation to generation.

It is probably apparent that what might be called a transference in my relationship with Tracy was not eliminated by any interpretation or intervention on my part. Our trauma-generated so-called "idealizing transference" dissolved after Tracy and I were able to confront one another as mutually vulnerable to the repugnance of others – a repugnance she had lived with all her life. With the resumption of the interweaving flow of *I-you-we world,* feelings and memories that had been barred from our engagement now colored every moment we spent together. Although we had many difficult moments in the months that followed, a narrative involving a new way of being both vulnerable and strong in the face of societal antagonism could now come into being.

We hope that this clinical example demonstrates that what has been known as transference comes into being on the heels of the revival of traumatic memories. At such times, the complex interweaving of experience is stilled, and the vitality of ongoing narrative is greatly reduced. It is hard to predict when the remarkable power that is embodied by the therapeutic partners reinstates the flow of *I-you-we-world*, but its healing effects are rarely in doubt.

References

Brothers, D. (2016). Screams and shouts: Trauma, uncertainty, and the ethical turn. In D. Goodman & E. Severson (Eds.), *The ethical turn: Otherness and subjectivity in contemporary psychoanalysis*. London, England and New York: Routledge.

Damasio, A. R. (2010). *Self comes to mind*. London, England: William Heinemann.

Freud, S., & Breuer, J. (1893/95/1955). Studies on hysteria. In J. Strachey (Ed. & Trans.), *The standard edition of the complete psychological works of sigmund freud* (Vol. 2, pp. 1–251). London, England: The Hogarth Press.

Levinas, E. (1947/1987). *Time and the other*. (R. Cohen Trans.). Pittsburgh, PA: Duquesne.

Lichtenberg, J. (2017). The dialogic nature of narrative in creativity and the psychoanalytic dialogue. In J. D. Lichtenberg, F. M. Lachmann & J. Fosshage (Eds.), *Narrative and meaning: The foundation of mind, creativity, and the psychoanalytic dialogue*. London, England and New York: Routledge.

Schacter, D. L. (1996). *Searching for memory*. New York: Basic Books.

Schafer, R. (1976). *A new language for psychoanalysis*. New Haven, CT and London: Yale University Press.

Stolorow, R. D. (2011). *World, affectivity, trauma: Heidegger and post-Cartesian psychoanalysis*. New York: Routledge.

Chapter 6

Resistance or the lack of freedom to change?

"What brings you here today?" Even if analysts don't verbally pose this question to patients who come for their first analytic sessions, it invariably hangs in the air. The answers may be as vague as "things aren't going well for me," or as specific as, "I no longer love my spouse but cannot end my marriage," or "I need to lose weight," but they usually indicate some desire for change – change in one's life situation, or in one's relationship, or in one's body, or in one's habits, or even in one's entire self.

It is consequently assumed by both analytic partners that the patient has chosen to change. Even patients who hope to be "fixed" by their analysts enter treatment with the expectation of having to make some sort of life changes. But making changes in one's life requires agency, or the intention to act. And as anyone who has worked therapeutically knows, changing is far easier said than done. Freudians viewed the reluctance to change in terms of drive-theory notions of resistance and defense. Although few contemporary analysts imagine that their patients continually fight against id impulses of a sexual or aggressive nature that press for discharge, there has been little consensus regarding the problematic nature of therapeutic change.

In this chapter we examine two possible reasons for the wrenching difficulty so often encountered in attaining therapeutic change. First, desirable as it might seem to be, the sense of being free to change is often experienced as terrifyingly fraught with danger. This is particularly true of patients who have come to believe that their going-on-being depends on their clinging to inflexible relational patterns. Secondly, what we are calling "subtle neurological conditions," such as "attention deficit hyperactivity disorder" (ADHD) or "high-functioning autism," may greatly impede the change process.

Our clinical finding that analytic relationships based on *we*-connectedness makes change more readily attainable for such patients raises questions about the usefulness of the concept of resistance. We suggest that the very word, "resistance," connotes an unwillingness to change. In contrast, we will try to show that many patients who might once have been deemed "resistant" lack a sense of freedom to change, a sense of agency. Many contemporary analysts would probably agree with Kohut (1984), who understood resistance and

DOI: 10.4324/9781003265047-7

defense as activities undertaken in the service of "psychological survival." We see that the development of a greater sense of certainty about one's going-on-being as well as a greater toleration of life's irreducible uncertainty are necessary accompaniments to feeling free to change. We believe that certain constitutional factors also greatly affect one's sense of freedom to change.

Although Freud famously claimed that, because we are at the mercy of unconscious drives and motives, we lack free will, many philosophers and theologians have argued that free will is the basis for civilization as we know it. This contention is problematic to the extent that it is often tied to a Cartesian view of individuals as solitary and rational. As Roger Frie expressed the Cartesian viewpoint: "I think, *I choose*, therefore I am" (2008, p. 378).

The impossibility of free will has also been advanced by neuroscientists who claim that our brains commit to certain decisions before we are aware of having made them (e.g., Damasio, 2010). Many contemporary psychoanalysts, in contrast, are less concerned with the neurological limits of our free will than with our experience or sense of being free to act and change, as well as our experience of being unfree. Harry Stack Sullivan (1950), an early proponent of the idea that self-experience is always relationally generated, has written: "I know of no evidence of a force or power that may be called a *will*" (p. 191).

As Boulanger (2007) reminds us, the earliest expression of personal agency is experienced as control over one's motor behavior. In the throes of what will become a traumatic experience, we often feel unable to will ourselves to exert control over our bodily movements. Feelings of being frozen in place or paralyzed are common (see Chapter 2 on the slowing or freezing of the *I-you-we-world* flow). Moreover, the ability to will oneself not to relive a traumatic experience is just as impossible as willing oneself to recall a traumatic experience that has been dissociated from conscious memory.

In what follows, we view the fear and dread associated with the freedom to change through the lens of the psychoanalytic understanding of trauma we have been developing in this book. Because posttraumatic experiential modes such as *I*-centeredness or *you*-centeredness were once desperately needed to overcome the anguish of trauma (see Chapter 3), they are clung to even after one's going-on-being no longer depends on them. Thus, the very notion of change means relinquishing the ways of being in the world that allowed one to moderate the unbearable feelings associated with traumatic helplessness and uncertainty.

Clinicians often notice that as patients make gains in treatment, they report more anxiety. We believe such anxiety is a natural consequence of relinquishing the certainty-maintaining strategies that were once felt to be the only protection against re-experiencing traumatic terror. Yet, without finding the courage to live without these constricting modes, patients may never experience the sense of freedom required for change. Such freedom, we believe, arises within the embodied sense of *we*-connectedness that develops between some analysts and patients.

Although it is usually the patient who is expected to change, there is growing recognition that no substantial healing takes place if the analyst fails to change as well. However, when the analyst's own memories of trauma are revived in the analytic relationship, the analyst's fear of change may also work to impede therapeutic recovery. It is our contention that when *we*-connectedness is enhanced within the therapeutic exchange, both members of the analytic partnership are likely to become less fearful of change.

Why does the sense of *we*-ness that underlies the capacity for agentic change require the body-to-body feeling connection of patient and analyst? Wilhelm Reich suggested a reason for this by noting that "the latent negative transference," or "secret resistance," was not expressed in the context of words, but rather "in the way the patient speaks, looks at and greets the analyst, lies on the couch, the inflection of the voice, the degree of conventional politeness which is maintained" (1933/49/72, p. 49).

We also believe that Roger Frie (2008) has pointed to the answer in his focus on "the fundamental embodiment of the agentic process" (p. 367). He draws on Merleau-Ponty's (1962) understanding that the body is "the visible form of our intentions" (p. 5), the assertion of Lakoff and Johnson (1999) that the body's preconceptual meaning structure provides the basis for our metaphors about time and space, and the neurological research of Antonio Damasio (1994). Frie underlines the complex nature of agency. He asserts that choice is never an isolated act, but rather "a complex process of reflection, informed by personal history and fundamentally embedded in biological and sociocultural contexts" (p. 373). It is his observations that "the patient's and the analyst's bodily experiences are always implicit in the discourse of the clinical setting" (p. 373) and, consequently in agentic change, that we now want to elaborate upon.

We believe that it is precisely the embodiment of *we*-connectedness that allows the analytic partners to tolerate – if not welcome – change to the extent that their developing closeness provides a sense of safety in which to experience all of their feelings – no matter how conflictual they might be.

In the clinical example that follows, we attempt to show how agentic terror may be relieved through embodied contact. This patient's struggle with her mother stirred painful memories of a similar nature for Doris that proved disruptive to the *I-you-we-world* flow of their embodied exchange.

Doris and Jen

Jen raced into my (Doris') office for our first session as if she had been chased. Even before she dove into her seat, Jen's eyes urgently sought mine and I held her intense gaze with my own. I remember imagining that if I looked away – even for a moment – I would send her plummeting into some hellish void. She explained that she feared she was entering a period of utter disintegration like the ones that had recurred at the same time (early spring) for the past few years. Although she had been at the top of her class in college and was doing well in her first job, she nevertheless lived in dread of failing. The only relief for her crippling anxiety and despair came during frequent phone calls with her mother.

Jen described her mother as an empathic and caring woman who suffered from a painful illness that severely constricted her life. The way Jen described both her father's devotion to his wife as well as her own feelings for her mother called to mind the experience of some family members of Holocaust survivors I have known. Because no suffering of theirs could come close to the pain felt by the survivor, they felt compelled to do everything in their power to ease that unimaginable pain.

After we worked together for several months, Jen gradually emerged from her crippling distress and energetically began to prepare for the entrance exam required for graduate schools. Although the pandemic forced us to switch to Zoom sessions, we easily developed a mutual sense of embodied relating. Jen seemed to respond to my facial expressions and gestures as easily and fluently as I did to hers. I felt the exhilaration that comes from closely synchronized body-to-body connectedness, much like a dance in which neither partner leads nor follows – a feeling no words can adequately convey. Our worded dialogues were often full of playful wit and our silences dense with feeling.

We had come to believe that Jen's periodic distress was connected to her need to protect against feelings of guilt and shame for failing to achieve some goal her mother had silently selected for her. Since acceptances to many of the programs and jobs she had previously applied for were announced in the spring, we imagined that her fear of failing to gain acceptance had triggered these repetitive periods of anxiety and depression.

I hoped that, since our explorations of this relational configuration seemed to allow Jen to experience greater freedom to choose a path congruent with her own needs and ambitions, she would not experience a recurrence of symptoms this year. However, as the second wave of the pandemic struck, Jen became consumed with worry that her mother would become fatally ill with COVID. Consequently, Jen's contacts with her mother resumed their previous frequency and intensity.

To my dismay, when spring arrived, so did Jen's distress. As she withdrew into her anguished self-involvement, I was flooded with memories of my own painful struggles to find a career path different from the one my own mother had chosen for me.

The moment we have selected to examine from our embodied perspective occurred when, fearing that the periodicity and severity of Jen's symptoms indicated a need for antidepressant medication, I suggested that Jen consult a psychiatrist. She tearfully accused me of giving up hope that our work together would help her.

The "I" position

I (Doris) am aware of not wanting to look into Jen's eyes, but I don't know what I'm afraid of seeing in them. Our bodily movements have fallen out of sync and I'm filled with a sense that all the fluidity and gracefulness of our "dance" has disappeared. We even interrupt one another when we speak. All I can think about is the way I struggled to pursue my own life choices against my mother's wishes. Jen has disappeared.

The "you" position

I (Jen) collapse into myself and look away from the screen into my own lap. I feel the rising heat of anger in my chest as I lift my gaze to Doris' face. Seeing the stranger she has become, I fight the urge to cry. I want to shout, "Don't leave me. Come back!"

The "we" position

They are both feeling great distress at the deterioration of their once effortless body-to-body connectedness. The similarity of Doris' struggles to free herself from her mother's needs had made her withdraw from contact with Jen. Jen experienced Doris as abandoning her for clinging to her mother rather than choosing her own path. Her dread that she must comply with the needs of the other or lose her had been reinforced.

I decided to tell Jen that because our work had reminded me of my painful struggles to find my own life path against my mother's wishes, I had been unable to maintain my closeness to her. I wondered if I had not repeated her dilemma with her mother insofar as I had seemed to require her to meet my need for her to change. I acknowledged my unspoken wish for her to put her own needs ahead of her mother's, and suggested that doing so would have put her at great risk. Instead of diminishing my helpfulness as a therapist in Jen's eyes, my self-disclosure seems to have convinced her that since I had managed to free myself from my bondage to my mother, I could help her achieve the same freedom.

Almost immediately our embodied interactions resumed their effortless flow. As Jen sensed that I had not lost hope in our work, she once again emerged from her lonely torment. Although we still cannot be certain that Jen's periodic periods of depression and anxiety will not recur, with each passing month we both feel that Jen is enjoying greater and greater freedom to choose her own life path.

Constitutional factors affecting freedom to change

So far, we have only mentioned how the need to restore a sense of certainty in the aftermath of trauma may interfere with one's freedom to change. We have suggested that a patient's reluctance to relinquish ways of being in the world, that seemed to offer a sense of certainty about going on being, has often been regarded as resistance in psychoanalytic treatment. However, we now introduce the idea that many constitutional factors may also play a role in so-called resistance to change.

Among these factors are the ways in which physical appearance affects the interpenetrating flow of *I-you-we-world* between the analytic partners. If we are correct that one's sense of courage to change depends on the quality of the embodied contact of the analytic partners, then race and ethnicity, physical health and disability as well as perceived beauty must greatly influence the connectedness of the analytic partners.

We also suspect that what we call "subtle neurological conditions" affect the sense of freedom to change. Among patients suffering from these conditions are those viewed as falling somewhere on the autism spectrum or who receive diagnoses of ADHD. However, as our clinical examples hopefully demonstrate, it is virtually impossible to separate traumatic experiences and constitutional factors because they tend to become so entangled in a person's life.

The flow of *I, you, we* and *world* among patients suffering from subtle neurological conditions is unlikely to be fluid. In fact, many of them might be considered *I*-centered to the extent that they seem preoccupied with themselves and bemoan their difficulties in relating to others. However, few of those we have treated resemble the *I*-centered patients who are thought of as grandiose and self-referential. Since experiencing a sense of freedom to change is particularly problematic for these patients, it is hardly surprising that many traditional analysts regarded them as "unanalyzable." Even for contemporary analysts who attempt to treat such patients, the challenges involved may be daunting.

Intense *I*-centeredness, difficulty in work and personal relationships as well as the entangling of traumatic experience and constitutional factors were very much the focus of Jon's analysis with a patient whom we call Lynn.

Jon and Lynn

When Lynn first sought therapy with me (Jon) in her early 20s, she complained that she had "lost contact" with herself and the world around her. She described herself as "living inside a thick fog" that prevented her from sharply distinguishing her own feelings and, consequently, making it impossible for her to sustain connections with others. Maintaining focus on her studies had proved so arduous that she had left university and had traveled abroad in the hope that doing so would "clarify her mind." But nothing she tried had helped and she had sunk into great despair marked by intense self-loathing. Her initial accounts of her childhood led us both to believe that her difficulties had been caused by severe physical and verbal abuse by her father.

There were many long periods during the ten years of her analysis in which Lynn hardly spoke at all. Although she often apologized for being "boring," she also let me know that it was extremely important to her that I remain close to her despite her silences. Since I felt strongly moved by her suffering, it was not difficult for me to do so. Gradually, by staying in close embodied contact with her – adjusting my expression and gestures in ways that matched hers – the fog seemed to lift, and she resumed and then eventually completed her studies in a mental health field. Even more rewarding for her was that she managed to enter what turned out to be an enduring relationship with a man and to have two children with him.

Almost ten years later, she called to ask to resume analysis. After several years of employment as a mental health worker, she had increasingly experienced symptoms of burnout. By the time she recontacted me, she had stopped working. I assumed that her work issues were somehow connected to her earlier problems. After some time, Lynn mentioned that she had become aware of literature on adult female ADHD that had not been recognized because the symptomatic picture differs greatly from the prototypical examples of young boys with ADHD. It was not the content of her complaints but the repetitive nature of them that I found to be similar to the descriptions of adult female ADHD in the literature. In what follows I describe a turning point in our therapeutic relationship.

The "I" position

I (Jon) feel increasingly alert and excited as I listen to Lynn's description of ADHD in adult women. I notice that she is closely watching my reactions to her words. Relief floods my body as I realize that she has finally provided us with the answers to questions about her functioning that had long troubled me. I feel that I must let her know what her account means to me.

The "you" position

I (Lynn) sigh with joyful relief as I perceive that Jon believes in what I am telling him about ADHD. I feel a renewed sense of closeness to him. For the first time I feel hope that I will escape from my self-imposed prison.

The "we" position

Their joint recognition of the relevance of "female adult ADHD" has filled them both with a renewed sense of purpose. They have found a shared language for Lynn's difficulties in living. Jon's willingness to open himself to Lynn's discovery also created a fresh, hopeful sense of **we**-connectedness.

After I had confirmed the value of what Lynn had researched on her own, we began a new chapter of our work together. We realized that, even in childhood, her behavior had been impulsive and that she had experienced difficulties with self-control. Although she still struggles with impulsive and repetitive reactions, especially when she is angry, she feels more compassion with her occasional failures in self-control.

We now consider how what is now termed, "high-functioning autism," may affect one's sense of freedom to change. We start by reviewing the history of the disorder that was once called "Asperger's syndrome."

About "Asperger's"

In 1944, an Austrian pediatrician named Hans Asperger described four young patients with similar social difficulties. Although their intelligence appeared normal, the children lacked nonverbal communication skills and failed to demonstrate empathy with their peers. Their manner of speech was either disjointed or overly formal, and their all-absorbing interests in narrow topics dominated their conversations. The children also shared a tendency to be clumsy (Barahona-Correa & Filipe, 2015).

Dr. Asperger's observations, published in German, remained little known until 1981. In that year, the English physician Lorna Wing published a series of case studies of children with similar symptoms. Wing's (1981) writings on "Asperger syndrome" were widely published and popularized. In 1994, Asperger syndrome was added to the fourth edition of the Diagnostic and Statistical Manual of Mental Disorders (DSM-4), the American Psychiatric Association's diagnostic reference book.

While some patients welcome the diagnosis of Asperger syndrome, or high-functioning autism as it is now called, insofar as it provides a way for them to understand the difficulties they face in their lives, we believe that others are likely to suffer negative effects from being placed in this diagnostic category. These individuals may feel that they have been distinguished from other human beings who inhabit a welcoming, accepting world where their idiosyncrasies are regarded as indications of their uniqueness. While others are regarded as quirky or whimsical or as being "characters," those who are deemed to be "on the spectrum" are viewed through a pathological lens (see Chapter 7 on the *Us-them* Binary).

On the autism spectrum

Few psychoanalysts practicing in the 1990s were likely to welcome adults into their practices who suffered from "high-functioning autism," and, who, more colloquially, are said to be "on the spectrum." Sugarman (2011) suggests three possible reasons for the erroneous belief that such patients would not benefit from analytic treatment. First are the now discredited claims by analysts writing in the 1950s and 1960s that poor parenting is responsible for the condition. Although Leo Kanner, writing in 1943, had identified "Early Infantile Autism" as a disorder marked by "an inborn disturbance in affective contact," some well-regarded analysts such as Bergman and Escalona (1949), Margaret Mahler (1952, 1968) and Bruno Bettleheim (1972) had suggested that it might be the result of disturbances in early interactions between mothers and infants (Bettelheim, 1976). Bettlleheim (1972) notoriously blamed "icebox mothers."

Secondly, Sugarman points to the widely shared assumption that a bio-chemically based disorder cannot by treated analytically. Even today there is a great deal of literature suggesting that only cognitive behavioral approaches are helpful. And thirdly, Sugarman identifies the lingering perception that psychoanalysis still prioritizes the uncovering of hidden, unconscious con-tents. Because people diagnosed as suffering from high-functioning autism are likely to have difficulties with processes known as "mentalizing," "affect regulation" and "social language," it was believed that attempts by analysts using traditional notions of cure designed to make them aware of the uncon-scious meanings of their thoughts, fears or fantasies would only confuse them or result in narcissistic injury.

In what follows, Doris describes her relationship with a young man she began working with before the diagnoses of "Asperger's syndrome" or "high-functioning autism" were commonly used.

Doris and Lyle

Moments after he entered my office for our first session, I realized that Lyle, a gangly 20-year-old man with a mop of curly hair tied into a long ponytail, was distinctly unlike anyone else I had ever worked with. When I asked him what had brought him to my office, Lyle answered, "A subway train." He then provided me with a virtual step-by-step account of the trip from his college dorm to my office. Stifling a giggle at what I initially took for his joke, Lyle's reaction told me that his reply was not meant to amuse me but to answer my question as precisely as he possibly could. He then let me know that he was aware that I had misinterpreted his comments as an attempt to be funny. "I have an oddball sense of humor," he said, "but I wasn't trying to make you laugh just now. A lot of people don't seem to know when I'm being funny and when I'm being serious."

In fact, I learned that many people who became acquainted with Lyle – he had no friends – felt much as I did: they didn't know what to make of him. He was full of contradictions. Clearly brilliant in his academic studies, especially in math and science, and a talented musician, he had not seemed to learn the basics of ordinary human interaction. He could describe in painstaking detail how others responded to him, but he could not predict in advance how his behavior might be perceived. Nor did his awareness of another's responses prompt him to alter his behavior in any way. Doing anything that required deviation from his narrowly regulated patterns of living overwhelmed him with anxiety. I later learned that it had taken him months to work up the courage to phone me for an appointment.

Lyle had sought therapy with me at the urging of a friend of his parents, a colleague of mine, after he had become virtually immobilized when a young woman in one of his classes rejected him. He told me that it had taken him months of agonizing indecision before he had managed to recite his carefully memorized script at the doorstep of the woman he would subsequently call, "Sue, Sex Goddess." Thrusting a bouquet of flowers at her, he asked if he could enter her dorm room to talk with her. "No," she had coldly responded as she unceremoniously slammed the door in his face. She had not even looked at the flowers he had finally decided were exactly the right ones to give to her on Valentine's Day. Lyle spent the following weeks, if not months, of sessions examining every conceivable aspect of this shameful encounter. Sue was fair-skinned and red-haired and had nostrils shaped in exactly the way that captivated Lyle.

Since I was not familiar with the concept of high-functioning autism at the time I began working with Lyle, I could not imagine what had led Lyle to experience life and other people in this idiosyncratic way. Lyle's answers to my questions about his background were concrete and superficial. He described his parents as highly intelligent people who had achieved considerable success in their careers. According to Lyle, they had understandably expected that he would follow in their footsteps and make his own mark in the world.

His parents, according to Lyle, concerned about his social awkwardness, had taken him to see many therapists and school guidance counselors. Asked how that was for him, Lyle said that he had liked playing games with them and some of them laughed at his jokes. "I never thought it would do any good, but I didn't mind going," he admitted.

At first, our twice-weekly sessions were dominated by Lyle's very detailed monologues about such quotidian events as the television programs he watched, or his struggle to order food from the local pizzeria or to phone for a doctor's appointment. The only emotion he seemed able to describe was anxiety. And just about anything that required his moving out of his highly circumscribed routine made him anxious. For months, realizing that he would talk right over most of what I tried to say, I simply listened quietly to him. I eventually began to murmur in response to his remarks, and then to make short comments. By the end of the second year, he seemed better able to tolerate my efforts at empathic communication and would occasionally stop talking long enough to make room for my reactions.

I discovered that the more accurately I captured the feelings that Lyle had not described in his verbal accounts, the more effort he subsequently seemed to make in relating the emotional contexts of his experience. I wondered if I were modeling an aspect of experience that he had previously disregarded.

Lyle also responded positively when I described aspects of my own emotional reactions to situations that resembled ones he had described. I would provide detailed accounts of my feelings of shame, anger, sadness, or resentment and so on in similar circumstances. I also discovered that he would listen intently whenever I described my reactions to his verbalizations, such as, "I felt sad when you told me about your grandmother's funeral." It was only when I provided these emotionally descriptive responses that Lyle asked me questions about my experiences. What exactly was it that had prompted my feeling, he would ask. Aside from the interest he showed at such times, he seemed remarkably disinterested in learning anything else about me. I have probably disclosed less about myself to Lyle than to any other of my long-term patients.

The glacial slowness of what I perceived to be positive movement both in the development of our relationship as well as in Lyle's life proved quite daunting for me at times. I worried about not having found a way to reach him. Colleagues I consulted more or less scratched their heads in bewilderment. Then, to my relief, sometime in the third year, Lyle began to describe aspects of the emotional context of his early life. I learned, for example, that Lyle's father had a ferocious temper that could flare up unpredictably. His mother, intimidated by her husband, seemed to have worked hard to appease him. Lyle mentioned that he found that his father's reasoning was likely to be "faulty" when he shouted. He then described how contradicting other people for what he found to be "faulty reasoning" often got him into trouble.

Curiously, Lyle never contradicted me or argued with me about anything I said. Perhaps this was because I tried to stay as close as I could to Lyle's experience and refrained from interpreting his behavior. Since I was in the dark about what had organized his experience in this odd way, I had not even hoped to be able to enlighten him. At this point, I did not feel that Lyle and I shared what I consider *we*-connectedness, but I have wondered if it was some sort of body-to-body resonance that enabled us to form a sort of proto we-connectedness.

In retrospect, I have come to believe that something of a turning point occurred in our relationship when Lyle disclosed that he habitually masturbated to pornographic videos, especially those involving sadomasochistic sexuality (they were not yet available on the internet). I said something to the effect that I could appreciate how exciting and sexually stimulating they might be for him. "Yes," he said emphatically. "They are!" It is this session that I now use to illustrate our approach to describing clinical interactions.

The "I" position

I (Doris) feel tense and focused. Something in Lyle's manner seems to have informed me that he will reveal something especially meaningful. I attend to his facial expressions carefully and listen for changes in his tone of voice. As he blurts out that he has used sadomasochistic pornographic videos for masturbation, I feel my body become still. I worry that I will not respond in a way that communicates my acceptance and understanding. After finding words that seem to relieve him, I breathe deeply. My tenderness for him warms me.

The "*you*" position

I (Lyle) feel excited and brave. I have rehearsed telling Doris about my S&M masturbation, but it's frightening to think that she may be disappointed or even disgusted with me. I watch her face and movements closely to try to detect any dangerous signs. When she lets me know that she understands how gratifying these experiences are to me, I am flooded with good feeling for her.

The "*we*" position

Doris and Lyle are prepared for a meaningful interaction. While each is afraid of disappointing the other, both are also excited about what is about to happen. After their verbal exchange, they are enveloped in a sense of being joined in contact. It is as if a baby has fallen into the comfort of his mother's arms.

In the next session, Lyle addressed me directly for the first time: "You're different from my other therapists," he said. "How so?" I asked. "You don't try to get me to do things according to your ideas about what would be good for me," he said. "All my other therapists tried to get me to be more social and to mingle with other people. Every time I see my parents, they ask about what I'm doing to make friends. I guess I expected you to tell me to give up watching S&M videos and go out and date girls. But I'm glad you didn't."

After a four-year hiatus, while Lyle attended graduate school, he returned to therapy. The years that followed brought some remarkable changes in Lyle's life. Having published articles in leading journals in his field, Lyle was often asked to give talks about his work at conferences and scientific meetings. To his surprise and mine, Lyle proved to be extremely good at presenting his work. "I get to tell jokes and make people laugh," he confided. He also enjoyed the camaraderie that developed among the scientists who worked in his lab, and he occasionally went out to dinners with them.

He could now describe his interactions with people with surprising empathy. He began to date women in the lab and fell in love with one of them. To his great delight, she welcomed his sexual advances and seemed to enjoy deepening their relationship. I have recently received an invitation to their wedding.

I'm very glad that, when we met, so many years ago, I did not try to locate him "on the spectrum." He was simply a young man whose body spoke to mine.

We hope that we have shown how the development of strong *we*-connectedness between the analytic partners allows many patients for whom change is fraught with difficulty – whether on account of traumatic histories or subtle neurological conditions – to find the courage to do so.

References

Barahona, J. B., & Filipe, C. N. (2015). A concise history of asperger syndrome: The short reign of troublesome diagnosis. *Frontiers in Psychology*, *6*, 175. DOI: 10.3389/fpsyg.2015.02024

Bergman, P., & Escalona, S. K. (1949). Unusual sensitivities in very young children. *Psychoanalysis Study of the Child*, *4*, 333–352.

Bettelheim, B. (1972). *The empty fortress: Infantile autism and the birth of the self.* New York: The Free Press

Bettelheim, B. (1976). *The uses of enchantment.* London: Thames & Hudson.

Boulinger, G. (2007). *Wounded by reality: Understanding and treating adult-onset trauma.* Hillsdale, NJ: Analytic Press.

Damasio, A. R. (1994). *Descartes' error: Emotion, reason, and the human brain.* New York: Avon Books.

Damasio, A. R. (2010). *Self comes to mind.* London, England: William Heinemann.

Frie, R. (2008). Fundamentally embodied: The experience of psychological agency. *Contemporary Psychoanalysis*, *44*(3), 367–376.

Kanner, L. (1943). Autistic disturbances of affective contact. *Nervous Child*, *2*, 217–250.

Kohut, H. (1984). *How does analysis cure?* Chicago, IL: University of Chicago Press.

Lakoff, G., & Johnson, M. (1999). *Philosophy in the flesh.* New York: Basic books.

Mahler, M. S. (1952). On child psychosis and schizophrenia – Autistic and symbiotic infantile psychoses. *Psychoanal Study Child*, *7*, 286–305

Mahler, M. S. (1968). *On human symbioses and the vicissitudes of individuation.* New York: International Universities Press.

Merleau-Ponty, M. (1962). *The primacy of perception.* Evanston, IL: Northwestern University Press.

Sugarman, A. (2011). Psychoanalyzing a vulcan: The importance of mental organization in treating asperger's patients. *Psychoanal Inquiry*, *31*, 222–239.

Sullivan, H. (1950/1964). The illusion of personal individuality. In *The fusion of psychiatry and social science* (pp. 198–226). New York: Norton.

Wing, L. (1981). Asperger's syndrome: A clinical account. *Psychological Medicine*, *11*(1), 115–129.

Chapter 7

The us-them binary of fascist experience

This chapter reflects our deep concerns about *world* during the last decade. We regard the rise of ultra-nationalism and the ascendance of authoritarian leaders, which have marked these years, as posing dangerous threats to all we hold dear. In a recent article (Sletvold & Brothers, 2021) we described how a great deal of what we called "fascist experience" had infiltrated our lives and those of our patients. In what follows, we elaborate on these ideas and what we regard as the prevalence of an ominous us-them binary.

Erich Fromm expressed feelings similar to ours over 50 years ago. In his forward to the second edition of his 1941 book, *Escape from Freedom*, he explained that the fears that led to the rise of fascism "have not only continued but have greatly increased. . . . Modern man still is anxious and tempted to surrender his freedom to dictators of all kinds" (1969, p. xiii).

According to Jason Stanley (2021, p. xiv), political fascism includes many distinct elements: the mythic past, propaganda, anti-intellectualism, unreality, hierarchy, victimhood, law and order, sexual anxiety and appeals to the heartland. He also found striking similarities in the relationships of fascist leaders and their followers to those of patriarchal fathers and their families. But what most distinguishes fascist politics, according to Stanley, is its tendency to "separate a population into us and them," which leads to the dehumanization of those designated "them" (p. xv). He adds, "This limits the empathic capacity of other citizens and leads to the justification of inhumane treatment," which may, in extreme circumstances, result in "mass extermination" (p. xv).

Our main concern in this chapter is not on political fascism per se, but on the ways in which the us-them binary affects our daily lives and, at times, our psychoanalytic relationships. In our 2021 article, we suggested that no one is immune to the threat and temptations of fascist experience. We described our own vulnerability to the us-them binary that became unmistakably apparent in our work with patients who supported someone we regarded as a fascist-leaning leader – Donald Trump.

We do not mean to suggest that every instance of us-them relating is tantamount to fascist experience. However, as our clinical examples hopefully

DOI: 10.4324/9781003265047-8

demonstrate, the point at which interacting in terms of us and them becomes fascistic is not always easy to discern.

We find support for our view that vulnerability to the us-them binary of fascist experience pervades our world in Wilhelm Reich's masterful and prescient book, *The Mass Psychology of Fascism* (1933/1942). He writes:

> My character-analytic experiences have convinced me that there is not a single individual who does not bear the elements of fascist feeling and thinking in his structure.
>
> (Reich, 1933/1942, pp. xiii–xiv)

What might we all have in common that sets the stage for the us-them binary so prevalent in fascist experience? The answer, we believe, lies in the fact that we live in a traumatized and traumatizing world. Along with Zygmunt Baumann (2008), we believe that today's economic fears have been inflamed by the frantic swirl of our "liquid times." Nightmare terrors of being left behind are often stirred when others, who were not previously seen as threats to one's sense of dominance in society, such as minorities and women, seem to streak ahead, leaving one in the dust. Living through the many rapid-fire upheavals and changes of "liquid modernity," we cannot help being reminded of the terrifying uncertainty of our going-on-being.

It also seems likely to us that because the rapid changes of our liquid society have forced people to find economic opportunities far from their places of birth, communities have dissolved and bonds of friendship have been torn. Moreover, we live in a time in which body-to-body interactions have become less commonplace. Not only has the use of the internet become widespread – we shop, bank, even look for romantic partners online – but the COVID pandemic has forced us to further reduce our embodied contacts with others. This has increased our vulnerability to what Hannah Arendt (1951) called "radical loneliness." She described how this sort of loneliness sets the stage for the rise of authoritarian leaders. As part of a group of followers of a revered leader, loneliness may diminish. We see the radical loneliness of our times as increasing our sense of uncertainty about our going-on-being and concomitantly to our need for ways to reduce this uncertainty.

As we mentioned in Chapter 3, since complexity tends to increase the experience of uncertainty, we tend to search for ways to simplify our experience. The creation of binaries is a tried-and-true means of providing simple answers to complex questions, and no binary has more power over us than that of "us vs. them." Racism, sexism, xenophobia and virtually every form of political malevolence depends on it. We contend that fascist experience, which revolves largely around the us-them polarity, represents an extreme effort to find certainty in a world trembling with uncertainty.

When we-ness becomes "us vs. them"

A major contention in this book is that the fluid shifting between *I* and *you* creates a sense of *we*. After severe or longstanding traumatic experiences, our ability to create a sense of *we* may be severely damaged. Instead, *I*-centeredness or *you*-centeredness tend to dominate a person's relational world. At times of great societal stress, a sense of *we*, for some people, may be based only on sameness. This *we* then becomes "us," and all others who are not experienced as the same as us become "them." At such times, our embodied feelings change dramatically. When we feel connected to those we view as "us," we tend to experience a sense of calmness, safety, openness and even, at times, elation; when viewing ourselves with respect to those we consider "them," we tend to experience fear, hostility and withdrawal.

To our surprise, we discovered that in the novelist Karl Ove Knausgaard's (2011/19) explorations of Hitler's ideology, his understanding of fascist experience is remarkably similar to ours. He argues that language itself is a social activity that presupposes an "I" and a "you" that together makes a "we." To explain what underlies the fascistic *we*, he writes:

> What made the atrocities of the Third Reich possible was an extreme reinforcement of the we, and the attendant weakening of the I, which lessened the force of resistance against the gradual dehumanization and expulsion of the non-we, which is to say the Jews. . . . Within only a few years the voice of conscience in Germany went from thou shalt not kill to its reverse, thou shalt kill, as Hannah Arendt points out.
>
> (p. 513)

According to Knausgaard, the way this happened is displayed in its purest form in Hitler's *Mein Kampf,* "which contains no 'you,' only an 'I,' and a 'we,' which makes it possible to turn 'they' into 'it.' In 'you' was decency. In 'it' was evil. But it was 'we' who carried it out" (p. 882).

We believe that Knausgaard highlights the crucial distinction between a *we* that is based on *I and you*, and a *we* without a *you*. The former is shaped by an embodied connectedness to one or more other persons, as is the case in a real friendship. The *we* without a *you* (which we prefer to call "us") is exemplified by certain isolated individuals who rarely feel that they are connected to others except when they are in the presence of a fascist leader. At such times, they may experience a sense of us-them connectedness. Perhaps the most telling mark of fascist experience is when recognition of the other, the *you* who is seen as both like and unlike us, is lost. The other is simply *them*.

We now present our work with patients who forced us to confront our own need to resort to the us-them binary.

Doris and Ben

Ben, a young white man who was diagnosed as suffering from bipolar disorder, initially entered therapy to fulfill a court order. He had been arrested for injuring a companion when a verbal dispute devolved into physical violence. Viciously abused by an older brother, subjected to the raging outbursts of his alcoholic father, bullied in high school and stunned by the sudden death of his mother, the young man was also at the mercy of frequent and intense alternations of depression and mania. Adding to his suffering was severe muscle pain that he blamed on the cocktail of psychotropic medications prescribed by a psychiatrist, and which he frequently refused to take.

On entering treatment, he expressed contempt for my "soft-hearted-soft-headed" approach, which contrasted with his worshipful attitude toward Donald Trump as a "tough guy who can't be pushed around." He also subscribed to a number of far-right conspiracy theories, involving violent threats to the country supposedly posed by various minority groups.

Although his painful bodily symptoms were dramatically relieved following a session in which he broke into tears upon describing the death of his mother and confessing to sorely missing her, he insisted that "crying will not cure me – it just makes me more depressed." He abruptly left treatment when he understood that a deepening involvement in his therapeutic relationship might involve experiencing more painful feelings that he considers signs of weakness and vulnerability, and which (I supposed) might lead him to question the veracity of his political beliefs.

My reaction to his leaving was equal parts disappointment and relief. I had often experienced enormous tension in my body during my sessions with Ben. At times I would sit very still, echoing Ben's stiff, unmoving way of occupying his chair. Even the muscles in his face seemed to have been set in a perpetual scowl. At other times, I found myself using rather exaggerated gestures as I moved in my seat, perhaps as a way of encouraging him to loosen up.

Although I had felt a great sense of compassion for his traumatic suffering, I had often struggled with a strong desire to convince him that his views were wrongheaded and dangerous. When he ended the treatment, I congratulated myself on managing to keep my views to myself. It had not occurred to me that I was as locked into an us-them view of the political situation as Ben was. I felt as much disgust and contempt for those on the other side of the political divide as he did for those on mine.

It was only when Ben surprised me by returning to treatment that I became aware of the intensity with which I had held my "us-them" stance. Although Ben initially spoke much less frequently of his allegiance to Trump's views and his belief in conspiracy theories, he now seemed to experience me as embodying many of the qualities that he once attributed to Trump. He clearly saw me as not only uniquely qualified to help him, but also as influential and powerful in the world. "You are the only person on the planet who understands, me." "You are my only friend in the world." "I found out that you travel around the world giving talks. Lots of people look up to you."

I initially welcomed Ben's return and believed that working through his inevitable disappointments in his idealized view of me would further his healing. However, as the intensity of his somatic symptoms diminished and his moods became more stable, he once again became intensely interested in politics. Enraged by the impeachment hearings, Ben spoke mockingly of the desperate "witch hunt" undertaken by Trump's opponents. He seemed to forget that he had once reviled me as "a soft-headed liberal shrink" and now spoke as if I shared his political views. When he announced that he had begun to volunteer with an ultra-right-wing group to promote Trump's reelection, feelings of rage and contempt overtook me. My compassion dissolved and I wondered if I could go on working with him. Should I remind him that I was opposed to everything the group represented, I wondered?

I now present a moment in my relationship with Ben using the *I, you* and *we* positions we outlined in Chapter 1 that revealed my vulnerability to us-them experiencing.

The "*I*" position

My (Doris') jaw is clenched and the muscles in my arms are tense. I hold myself very still as if any movement on my part would lead me to strike out at Ben. I am unable to think clearly about what has been going on in the session.

The "*you*" position

I (Ben) am suddenly strong again. No more the scared little kid, I'm a big man now. I can show Doris that tears and grief are for weaklings. I will convince her that I know the truth and that she is wrong to believe in her crazy New York lefty ideas.

The "*we*" position

Ben and Doris are equally armed against each other. They are bent on triumphing over the other to claim victory for their own perspectives. They have never been so physically out of synch. Doris' body is tight and folded in on itself while Ben's is full of swooping gestures. Doris' face is blank while Ben's is wreathed in smiles.

It was only after the storm of my outrage subsided that it struck me that my strongly held political convictions, although diametrically opposed to those held by Ben, were leading me into the neighborhood of "us and them." For example, I was as little interested in opening myself to arguments favored by Trump's supporters as Ben was in listening to arguments against these views.

I was as blinded by my strong emotions, which included rage and shame, as he was. And, while I had not submitted myself to an authoritarian leader, as Ben had done, I no longer felt that I was as immune to the seduction of someone who would give voice to my deeply held convictions as I had once believed.

What distinguished my reaction from Ben's was my willingness to reflect on my experience, his experience, (albeit my sense of *you* was barely present at times) and to consider our relationship, our growing sense of we-ness.

There is no happy ending to our story. Ben continues to leave and return to treatment every few months. Yet I am hopeful that a very slow deepening of our *we*-connectedness will also diminish our mutual vulnerability to the us-them polarity.

Jon and Tom

Tom, a lawyer working with a prestigious consulting firm, requested therapy to help him overcome experiences of incapacitating burnout. He mentioned emotional conflicts in interpersonal relationships, which I (Jon) soon came to attribute to a complicated trauma history involving his emotionally disturbed parents. Because of his intense anxiety, muscular tensions and body pain, I helped him attend to bodily tensions and reactions in sessions.

To my chagrin, however, Tom spent much time in his sessions expressing his admiration for Trump and his anger and contempt for what he referred to as "the extremely stupid liberal and leftwing cultural elite." Initially I was at a loss as to how I might respond. Since I see myself as liberal and left leaning, I felt personally challenged by his views. At the same time, I was afraid that if I openly voiced my opposition to them, our *we*-connection would break down. I feared that the analysis would turn into a political discussion and attention would be drawn away from Tom's pressing concerns. At the same time, I wondered if his need for certainty, his maintenance of an "us-them" dichotomy and his antagonism toward political enemies might partially be a consequence of his trauma history. Given these considerations, I decided to postpone raising the matter of our political disagreements.

The session I highlight now revealed much about what had been going on between us.

The "I" position

I (Jon) feel that I am having two almost diametrically opposed feelings. On the one hand, I'm filled with violent disgust for Tom's diatribes against immigrants whom he sees as draining society's resources and his exaltation of Trump's power. On the other, I feel great compassion for his struggles with critical and demeaning parents who had little time for his feelings. I hold my body still, unable to move freely. I cannot allow my movements to echo his.

The "*you*" position

I (Tom) am furious with Jon for his barely disguised opposition to my political views. It is obvious to me that he is like all those I despise for being soft on the worthless elements of society. I cannot bear his silent dismissal of all that matters to me just as my parents did. I must get rid of him as I was forced to free myself of my parents. My body is stiff with contempt for Jon.

The "*we*" position

Jon and Tom have barely formed a **we**-connection. Their bodies move without any joint rhythm and their conversations remain superficial. Nothing that matters to either of them has been given voice.

In the next session Tom abruptly decided to terminate treatment, citing "changed priorities" in his life. However, I now believe that his decision to terminate was largely caused by our unaddressed conflict of values. After the treatment ended, I realized that I had experienced much more resentment and anger about Tom's attitudes than I had allowed myself to feel consciously during our work together. I now imagine that he had become aware of my feelings insofar as they were transmitted bodily rather than through words.

Thinking about our relationship in hindsight, it also strikes me that I was one-sidedly focused on his subjective complaints at the expense of a focus on our emotional connectedness. Although he talked about feeling emotionally disconnected from other people, I was reluctant to explore our disconnectedness. I now suspect that I failed to call attention to our differences because I had avoided focusing on his bodily appearance. He had an oddly elegant posture and way of dressing that called to mind photos I have seen of "Hitlerjugend." Because this perception put me in touch with my abhorrence of Nazism, it may well have interfered with my attempts to empathize with his predicament.

There is no way of knowing what would have happened if I had been more aware of my complicated and negative feelings, my own embodied sense of "us vs. them," but I have little doubt that it contributed to the premature termination.

Embodied dialogues as the alternative to us vs. them

Our relationships with Ben and Tom put us in touch with the ease with which strongly held political feelings can lead to moralistic us-them experiencing. Our deep commitment to work for the good of our patients was overpowered by moral outrage at the fascistic strategies employed by Donald Trump, whom both of our patients idealized. Neither of us believes that adopting a relativistic posture based on moral neutrality was a viable alternative. Doing so would have precluded us from engaging in the possibility of future dialogues with our patients about our differing relationships to the world – even if doing so might involve arguing with them.

Our clinical examples demonstrate that when the **us-them** binary dominates the therapeutic relationship, there is little room for genuine dialogue that may involve differences of opinion. We believe that we can learn much from what Reich (1933) wrote about fascist experience. He makes the point that the success of a fascist movement does not rest on its use of arguments, and, for that reason, it cannot be reached with arguments. He notes that the rally speeches of the National Socialists (Nazis) given between the years of 1928 and1933 were "very conspicuous for their skillfulness in operating upon the *emotions* of the individuals in the masses and of avoiding relevant arguments as much as possible" (Reich,1933, p. 34, italics in the original). Similarly, Jason Stanley (2018) writes: "It is a core tenet of fascist politics that the goal of oratory should not be to convince the intellect, but to sway the will." He found the following quote by an anonymous author in a 1925 Italian fascist magazine: "The mysticism of Fascism is the proof of its triumph. Reasoning does not attract, emotion does" (p. 55). And in his last book, *Dear Zealots*, Amos Oz (2018) who writes about what he calls "fanaticism" in ways that are interchangeable with what we are calling fascist experience, simply states: "The fanatic does not argue" (p. 3). Later he adds:

> It is not the volume that defines you as a fanatic, but rather, primarily, your tolerance – or lack thereof – for your opponents' voices.
>
> (Oz, 2019, p. 14)

Developing tolerance for our patients' voices and their embodied communications when what they say runs afoul of our deeply held beliefs is undoubtedly worth striving for. Doing so makes for dialogue. As Donna Orange (2010) writes: "In a genuine dialogue people do attempt to convince each other, but they always listen with the expectation that the other can teach them something. Under this condition, understanding can emerge in the play of conversation" (pp. 104–105). Much as we agree with this statement, we have found that maintaining genuine dialogues based on embodied **we**-connectedness with patients in thrall to fascist leaders to be one of the greatest challenges in our work.

Us and them in psychoanalysis

The ability to negotiate differences with our patient in the context of honest dialogue is exactly what some analysts have called for. For example, Lewis Aron (1996), referring to Martin Buber's writings on the "interhuman," observes that an emphasis on mutuality and negotiation does not mean that discord should be minimized between patient and analyst.

While many analysts would probably share our belief that genuine dialogue based on tolerance for difference and discord is the alternative to the us-them binary, we find that psychoanalysis itself is still caught in its iron grip. Since Freud's time, no unifying sense of *we* connectedness has developed among the various groups that fall under the psychoanalytic umbrella. Strong us-them divisions, some quite hostile and contentious, have arisen among Freudians, Kleinians, Jungians, Adlerians, self-psychologists, and interpersonalists. While there are many relational analysts who have joined both the International Association of Psychoanalytic Self Psychology (IAPSP) and the International Association of Relational Psychoanalysis and Psychotherapy (IARPP), there have been few efforts to create joint conferences or workshops.

We suspect that one reason for the maintenance of such us-them divisiveness is that, in addition to living in a world filled with strife and upheaval, a great many people who become analysts have experienced traumas themselves or have parents and/or grandparents who have endured either personal or societal traumas. In their superb book, *History Beyond Trauma*, Davoine and Guadilliere (2004) examine the war-torn lives of many early psychoanalytic leaders. It seems likely to us that, along with their rich theoretical legacy, there are remnants of their efforts to come to terms with horrendous societal traumas, notably, the Holocaust, that relied on us-them relating.

We also find that the binary of us and them pervades psychoanalytic practices. First, the very category of patient is loaded with *them* meanings. While much lip service has been paid to the idea that analysts are "wounded healers," patients are often regarded, sometimes justifiably so, as the more severely wounded members of the analytic partnership. They suffer from developmental arrests, neurotic conflicts, all sorts of constitutional ailments and occupy various niches "on the spectrum." Such afflictions are rarely acknowledged by analysts as having anything to do with themselves. Freud seems to have tried to dismantle this binary to some extent. By proposing that all aspiring psychoanalysts should undergo psychoanalysis themselves, he suggested that we suffer from many of the same problems in living as our patients.

Despite the admittedly asymmetrical relationship formed by patients in need of help for their suffering and analysts whom they pay to provide it, the tendency to slip into us-them experiencing is subtly reinforced by many of the routines of our profession. For example, every time we fill out an insurance form with a DSM or ICD diagnosis, we implicitly reinforce the notion that only the patient has a diagnosable condition. While diagnosis is often valuable in determining what other forms of care a patient might require – including medication – it powerfully differentiates the one who diagnoses from the one who is diagnosed. We also believe that the power dynamics that differentiate the role of analyst from that of patient are intensified when the concept of "mental illness" permeates the therapeutic relationship. From his earliest publication in 1954 to his last project, *The History of Sexuality*, Michel Foucault was critical of attempts to apply psychiatric medical science to human personality (O'Farrell, 2005). And while other analysts have accepted his arguments, the concept endures. Malin Fors (2018) has extensively explored the power dynamics in psychoanalytic therapy.

It may not be possible – or even desirable – to eliminate all traces of us-them relating in analytic relationships. However, we suspect that the ways in which us-them veers into fascist experiencing can be greatly reduced when analysts become aware of how their bodies talk with their patients' bodies. In the next chapter we attempt to outline a supervision model that is designed to help therapists learn the language of embodiment. It may be that a viable alternative to the overwhelming seduction of "us and them" is embodied connectedness between ourselves and the other. Perhaps it is in this embodied sense of *we*-ness, constituted by *I* and *you*, that what Emanuel Levinas (1961) called "the face of the other" and what Martin Buber (1958) called "I and Thou," is to be found.

References

Arendt, H. (1951). *The origins of totalitarianism.* New York: Harcourt Brace Jovanovich.

Aron, L. (1996). *A meeting of minds.* Hillsdale, NJ: Analytic Press.

Baumann, Z. (2008). *Liquid times: Living in an age of uncertainty.* Cambridge: Polity

Buber, M. (1958). *I and thou* (Trans. R. Gregor Smith). New York: Charles Scribner & Sons.

Davoine, F., & Guadilliere, J. (2004). *History beyond trauma.* New York: Other Press.

Fors, M. (2018). *A grammar of power in psychotherapy: Exploring the dynamics of privilege.* Washington, DC: American Psychological Association.

Fromm, E. (1941/1969). *Escape from freedom.* New York: Henry Holt and Co.

Knausgaard, K. O. (2011/2019). *My struggle – Book six.* New York: Farrar, Straus and Giroux.

Levinas, (1961). *Totality and the other: An essay on exteriorty.* Duquesne: Duquesne University Press.

O'Farrell, C. (2005). *Michel Foucault.* Thousand Oaks, CA: Sage.

Oz, A. (2019). *Dear Zealots: Letters from a divided land.* Boston, MA and New York: Houghton Mifflin Harcourt.

Reich, W. (1933/1942). *The mass psychology of fascism.* New York: Farrar, Straus and Giroux.

Sletvold, J., & Brothers, D. (2021). The embodiment of us and them: Fascist experience in a traumatized world. *Ricerca Psicoanalitica, 2,* 359–371.

Stanley, J. (2018). *How Fascism works: The politics of us and them.* New York: Random House.

Chapter 8

Body-based supervision

In traditional psychoanalytic supervision, supervisors are expected to know how their supervisees should treat their patients. They are often called upon to explain how theory should be applied to the cases that are presented. While we have little doubt that traditional supervision has often been very helpful, our approach to supervision turns this model upside down. We do not believe that supervisors should be expected to know what is best either for the patients or for the supervisees themselves. For us, clinical knowledge and authority reside in the bodies of the supervisees and their patients. We believe it is our job as supervisors to find ways to help supervisees access this knowledge, which is often out of their conscious awareness.

Although we are guided as much by the theories that inform our work as traditional analysts are guided by theirs, we prefer to leave room for supervisees to decide which theories have the greatest explanatory value for the clinical situation they are considering.

Our approach is based on the model of embodied supervision that was developed at the Norwegian Character Analytic Institute and described in detail by Sletvold (2012, 2014). These writings also describe how body-based practices may be incorporated into psychoanalytic training programs that are usually concept-based. Over the last few years, we have elaborated on the original supervision model. Perhaps the most striking difference is that we include participants in group supervision whom we believe bring *world* to the original *I, you, we* design. Let us explain our approach:

We start by asking supervisees to provide a brief account of the patient and the progress of the therapeutic relationship, as is often done in traditional supervision. We then ask them to state what it is that they would like to explore in their work with the patient they have presented.

Next, we ask them to assume what we refer to as the *I* position. In this position the supervisees imagine being in a recent session with the patient. They are asked to "see" the patient again and to describe what they feel in their bodies when they do so as well as any thoughts, images, fantasies, etc., that arise.

DOI: 10.4324/9781003265047-9

Then we ask them to assume the *you* position. Here they are asked to "become" their patient. They do so by imitating the patient as closely as possible. They are prompted to imitate the patient's facial expressions, gestures, ways of sitting and moving and even speaking. Nebbiosi and Federici (2008, 2022) describe imitating their patients following sessions in a way that resembles this position. Next, the supervisor addresses the supervisees as if they were the patient. The remarks made to the patient vary greatly depending on what the supervisors feel may be pertinent to the situation presented.

We want to emphasize that we do not believe that when the supervisee "becomes" the patient, what emerges is the truth about what the patient is experiencing. Rather it is what the supervisee has unconsciously felt that the patient is experiencing.

In the *we* position that follows, the supervisees are asked to reflect on the interaction between themselves and their patients while remembering their experiences in the *I* and *you* positions. We have often found that new ideas about what has been going on in the therapeutic situation emerge at this point. Supervisees may then be asked if they would like to experiment with their new understanding by imagining themselves to be with the patient again. Sometimes this involves changing their posture or distance from the patients, or the way they speak. But often this simply involves feeling something new about the situation.

In the original model, the supervisees were asked to move physically from the *I* position to the *you* position and then to the *we* position. This often involved moving among three chairs. During the pandemic, when most of our supervision was conducted online, we found it both awkward and unnecessary for supervisees to actually change seats. We discovered that supervisees found it easy to assume the different positions without needing to move from chair to chair.

When supervision is conducted in a group setting, *world* enters the supervisory setting more explicitly. As we see it, this occurs as the other group participants bring their own unique flow of *I-you-we-world* to the therapeutic situation presented and thereby increase the complexity, richness and even the beauty, mystery, and uncanniness for the supervisee.

After completing the *I-you-we* positions, the supervisee is asked to imitate the patient once again for a short time. All the other participants in the supervision group are instructed to "*become*" the therapists for the patient presented and to first attend to what they experience in their bodies, then to notice what feelings, thoughts, images and fantasies arise for them. They are instructed not to attempt to "supervise" the supervisee but to direct their comments to the supervisor. They may be asked to explain how they would work with the patient. The supervisee is often asked to comment on what each group participant contributes.

Supervision illustration 1 – Steve and Sarah

We now describe a supervision session with a group of eight clinicians who have been meeting with us on Zoom for the last two years. They come from several different countries on both sides of the Atlantic and are at different stages in their clinical development – some are quite experienced therapists while some are early in their careers. Judging from the openness and playfulness expressed among the participants, we believe that they have come to trust, respect and appreciate one another greatly.

In this Zoom session, which we recorded, a supervisee, whom we will call Steve, presented his work with Sarah, a young doctoral student in neuroscience, who had complained of severe obsessive-compulsive symptoms. Steve was worried that he was not helping Sarah enough and hoped to learn more about what was going on between him and his patient.

The "I" position

Steve first mentions an unusual feeling in his face – "as if I want to smile." He thinks this might have been related to his happiness at seeing Sarah. Then he feels a change that was like "holding back tears." He mentions that feeling "a tenderness come over me," and then some anxiety and excitement. He adds, "My whole body feels warm. I feel proud of Sarah – how hard she had worked to focus on her life dreams." He reports seeing images of her in which she felt alone despite being with close friends because she could not talk about her problems with them. Steve mentions that he also has a sense of being valued by Sarah and that she felt their work together was important, both of which he connected to the tears he had held back.

The supervisor mentions that what Steve reports seems to have little to do with his not feeling good enough. Before this, however, the supervisor had simply reflected back and condensed some of what Steve reported about his embodied reactions.

The "you" position

After imitating Sarah's way of sitting and the expression on her face, Steve speaks as if he were Sarah. As Sarah, he reports having become more obsessive despite having had a more relaxed week. She had been unable to write poetry or paint or do any of the things she loved. She would read the same sample exam questions over and over without being able to answer it. When asked how it was to report these experiences to Steve, she (Steve) said, "I don't know what I'd do if I didn't have his support. It's very grounding. Steve really listens. I look forward to our sessions and wish we had more of them."

The "we" position

Steve mentions feeling as if there is a glass wall between him and Sarah, much like the glass that separates visitors from prisoners in movies he's seen. "Everything is clear, but there is this thin transparent wall." He is concerned about whether he is helping Sarah, although she seemed "more relaxed, more grounded." Then he again mentions "the wall. . . . There is some kind of separation."

The supervisor points out that Steve's worry about his ability to help emerged again in this position.

Group responses

Next, the supervisor asks Steve to imitate Sarah once more so that the others in the group can experience what it might be like to be the therapist for Sarah.

One member of the group says that the word that captured his bodily feeling when he tried to become Sarah's therapist is "intimacy." He adds: "I feel as if I am in a deep connection between two people."

Other group participants had strikingly different reactions. One said, "I felt deep concern. . . . This person is hardly here. Like I'm talking to the tiniest part of this person. I ask myself, 'How much do I push? How much do I try to get more and how much do I try to keep her safe?' I found it very disturbing."

Another participant remarked, "I felt mesmerized, hypnotized like watching the opening of a flower. Anxiety came up. Love and affection for her. Tears came to my eyes, wanting to get closer to her."

An extraordinary moment occurred when one participant said she felt as if she were watching someone coming out from under water, "like watching a mermaid emerge or watching a fish in the aquarium. I started feeling dissociated myself . . . I don't think I'm even seen by Sarah."

Astonishingly, Steve remarked that Sarah had just gotten tattoos that all depict the ocean and schools of fish. And that, in fact, when she writes poetry, her pen name is the word for a school of fish.

Steve expressed gratitude for the groups' reactions to Sarah. He said that he was glad that they had confirmed his feeling that there was still a great distance between them. He added, "Maybe I don't have to be searching so hard for empathy. I just need to let go – to open more to her."

Supervision illustration 2 – Gene and Jane

Gene introduces his work with Jane by noting that his therapeutic relationship with her has been the longest one in his career. Now 40 years old, Jane had entered therapy when she was 18. He describes her as a highly intelligent woman who spoke "like a journalist." Her speech, he said, was well organized but boring. He had suspected that "she was hiding behind the words." In her early 30s, she suddenly lost her ability to speak after becoming involved in a sadistic relationship with a man. Gene remarks, "She made rageful sounds but had no words." When Jane regained her ability to express herself verbally, she spoke angrily about her work as a radio personality and about several of her other relationships. She subsequently expressed intense rage toward her mother who had given Jane a written piece describing her experience of being raped. Realizing that her mother had often demanded that she reverse roles with her, Jane became greatly distressed. Gene reports having stayed on the phone with Jane for two hours after she tearfully reported this. She was silent while he spoke soothingly to her. "I succeeded in talking to her heart," he says.

Gene's reason for wanting to present his work with Jane for supervision involved the two last sessions he had had with her. He had been astonished by the richness of the words they exchanged, which "seemed to come from nowhere." He reports having suddenly become "intensely sexually attracted to her." Then he confides, "I'm scared. Maybe it's time to end the treatment. I'm reminded of a painting of an old man in love with a beautiful young girl."

When the supervisor asks if he had ever had sexual feelings for Jane before, Gene suggested that perhaps his sexual feelings for Jane had always been there but had suddenly become clear to him.

The "I" position

I (Gene) see Jane as so beautiful – like she embodies the beauty of all women. I feel love in my heart for her. When the supervisor asks about any thoughts, images or fantasies he might have, Gene replies, "I imagine having an affair with her. It would be fun. I have the fantasy that Jane would become my therapeutic spouse, that we would become a couple, and that we could live together."

The "you" position

Gene speaks as if Jane were addressing him: "I always find you, Gene, to be a beautiful man. You make me feel secure as a woman. I am developing desire for you, and I enjoy being with you. You are the only man who allows me to be the woman I want to be. I love the way you are a man, your creativity. I know you desire me. Instead of trying to seduce you, I will charm you."

The supervisor asks Gene (as Jane) if Gene is frightening her. Gene (as Jane) answers: "No, he doesn't scare me, it excites me. He helps me to feel who I am. It's really okay that he desires me."

The "we" position

Gene reports, "They are in a special place with a special light enjoying their strong feelings. There is no place for guilt or judgment. They cultivate a silence that makes their feelings more intense, more sexual. They are developing a way to say goodbye and return to their personal lives."

Group responses

One participant remarks: "I felt a kind of sadness creeping in. Yet although fears of transgression and sadness remained, I had a bubbly, joyful feeling – innocent, childlike. But loss and sadness were in the background."

Responding, Gene says that it was a special gift to stay innocent and naïve about the first intimation of love. He mentions feeling as if he were "recovering something I had when I was a kid, who I was then."

Another participant says, "I felt such softness, not needing to be armed."

Still another comments, "I would not want to end. I feel something is happening that has to do with my being a container. I would want to see what is contained."

As the session ended, Gene remarks: "I don't have to decide right now if I will end the therapy. I can talk with Jane and see if there's more to develop. I am open to talking with her. I *have* to talk with her."

In the next group meeting, Gene was asked what had happened after the supervisory session. He remarked that the question of ending the treatment no longer seemed urgent, that he was content to continue his relationship with Jane to discover where it might take them.

Supervision with Chinese therapists

In 2018 we were invited to present our work in both Beijing and Shanghai, and in 2019 we were invited to return to Shanghai. While conducting supervision groups in person with Chinese therapists during our visits in China, we were impressed with the relative ease with which they tuned into their own bodily reactions and those of their patients. It did not seem to matter that all verbalizations during these meetings required translation.

When the pandemic made it impossible for us to return to China, our hosts asked if we would consider offering supervision to online groups. Although eager to work again with Chinese therapists, we felt anxious that meeting with our supervisees online with the added complication of needing all our verbal communications translated would make our work very difficult. Still, we decided to give it a try. To our delight, perhaps because of the skill these therapists showed in registering bodily feelings, our supervision model seemed to prove helpful. In addition, we learned a great deal. As the therapists worked with us, they often were reminded of images that reflected Chinese culture. In these ways we gained new experiences of *world*.

We found that several of the Chinese therapists used our model in a way that other therapists have not: they asked us for help in understanding what had led to a patient's leaving a therapeutic relationship. We now present one supervisory session that involved a patient who had left treatment.

Li and Sue

Li describes Sue as a 30-year-old woman whose initial complaint was that her mother-in-law was interfering in her relationship with her five-year-old daughter. She also mentioned problems in her relationship with her husband, especially that she felt "unable to enter into her husband's heart."

After only two sessions, the treatment was interrupted by the pandemic, and Li did not see Sue for six months. However, when the treatment was scheduled to resume, Sue failed to show up for several sessions. When she did return she often came late. After 25 sessions, Sue stopped coming without giving notice that she wanted to end the therapy. When Li was asked how she wanted to use the supervision session, she replied that initially she felt great compassion for Sue but has come to feel that "she is a person with terrible aggression." She added, "I want to better understand Sue and what made her end so abruptly."

Unlike members of our other supervision groups, members of the Chinese group provided us with translated reports of patients they wanted to present for supervisions. We now offer a condensed version of Li's report on Sue:

Sue's childhood was marked by the belief that she was an unwanted child. She felt disliked by her parents who neglected her both emotionally and materially. Sue was a very anxious child, who constantly feared being abandoned by her parents. She fiercely envied her three younger siblings whom she felt her parents preferred. After the last sibling was born, Sue's parents went to work, leaving Sue alone at home. She felt that her parents cared for her only when she was sick.

Although terrified of competition, Sue studied very hard in an attempt to please her parents and win their affection. She envied classmates who did better than her at school, and worried that she was not attractive enough to win attention and admiration from male classmates.

In college Sue suffered from severe insomnia and became highly anxious every time she took an exam. She continually felt under great pressure and worried that experiences of dizziness and "a floating feeling" indicated that she might have a mental breakdown. She managed to put herself through college, but her insomnia continued through her first two years at work.

Sue was introduced to her husband by a cousin. He pursued her with great passion and although Sue was not in love with him, she felt so unattractive and worthless she agreed to marry him. She gave birth to a daughter a year later. While grateful for the stability in her marriage, she resents her husband's lack of ambition and the increasing emotional distance between them.

Li was asked to report on her embodied feelings in the *I, you* and *we* positions.

The "*I*" position

I (Li) am frozen with fear when I look at Sue. My breath is shallow and I sit very still – like I am in a block of ice. I wonder if she will attack me again. I want to run away but I can't move.

The "*you*" position

I (Li as Sue) am holding tears back. I am angry with Li. I don't want to be vulnerable with her. I don't want to be here anymore.

When the supervisor asked what it is like for her to be with Li, Li as Sue answers, "I used to feel that she understood me and cared for me but she doesn't like me anymore."

The "*we*" position

We have stopped trusting one another and we are both afraid of being hurt. We don't want to be close. The connectedness we felt in the early sessions has disappeared.

Group responses

When asked to "become" Sue's therapist, many of the group members expressed the sense of being with a very frightened, hurt, traumatized woman. One group member said, "I feel that Sue's anger is covering great pain." Another group member said she felt like she was with a young baby who needed her mother.

In response to the group's comments, Li said that she now realized that Sue had experienced the disruption in sessions resulting from the pandemic as an abandonment, like those in her early life. She had needed reassurance that she would be warmly welcomed back. When Sue subsequently came late or missed sessions, possibly as a way to test Li's continued warm feelings for her, Li felt angry and disrespected. Sensing Li's anger, she dreaded re-experiencing the disregard and contempt her parents had shown her. To avoid these painful feelings, Sue had ended the treatment.

Li thanked the group and said she now realized that it was not only Sue who had been hurt and angry; she had become angry when Sue seemed indifferent to her efforts at empathy. She had not realized how the disruption created by the pandemic had recalled memories of Sue's painful childhood, or that Sue had needed her warmth and acceptance on her return.

Summary

The supervisory cases we have chosen to present are not very dramatic. Yet, we hope they illustrate the theory of embodied psychoanalysis we have attempted to describe in this book. That is, we assume that every human encounter is a meeting between foreign bodies. Just as we feel that we cannot know our patients completely, so we feel that we as supervisors should not expect to know our supervisees and their patients completely. However, as in any relationship, who we are and how we relate to our supervisees makes a significant difference. Supervisees are bound to experience the supervision process as more or less helpful depending on their feelings for the supervisor as well as others in the group.

We wonder if we have also managed to demonstrate that the words exchanged in supervision, as in any psychoanalytic relationship, do not tell the whole story. Rather, we believe that in the silence between the words, the bodies of supervisees, supervisors and fellow group members talk about what is therapeutically meaningful.

References

Nebbiosi, G., & Federici, S. (2022). Miming and clinical psychoanalysis: Enhancing our inter-subjective sensibility. *Psychoanalytic Inquiry, 42*(4), 266–277.

Nebbiosi, G., & Federico-Nebbiosi, S. (2008). We got rythms. In F. S. Anderson (Ed.), *Bodies in treatment. The unspoken dimension* (pp. 213–233). New York: The Analytic Press.

Sletvold, J. (2012). Training analysts to work with unconscious embodied expressions. *Psychoanalytic Dialogues, 22*, 410–429.

Sletvold, J. (2014). *The embodied analyst – From freud and reich to relationality*. London, England and New York: Routledge Taylor & Francis Group.

Chapter 9

Why not the body?

It seems likely that psychoanalysis has finally begun its "turn toward embodiment" (Brothers & Sletvold, 2022). But what kept psychoanalysts from pursuing Freud's quest to demonstrate the bodily basis of psychological life for so long? In this concluding chapter, we offer some possible explanations.

Perhaps one reason for the delay in recognizing the role of embodiment in psychoanalysis has to do with the ways in which people in western societies experience their bodies. Consider the questions Sam Anderson raises in an article in the *New York Times Magazine*:

> What is the human relationship to the body? Is it like a roommate? A pet? A twin? A teammate? A rival? A parasite? A host? Is the body our essential self, or is it just an outer shell – and if so, is it more like a clam shell (homegrown, enduring) or a hermit crab shell (adopted, temporary)? Is it closer to a tamale husk or a hot dog bun or a pita pocket or the fluorescent cake-tube that wraps a Twinkie's sweet cream center? Is the body the other side of the coin of the mind, or is the body the whole coin itself, and is the mind just the series of images and slogans stamped, superficially, on the exterior? Is the body an ancient piece of hardware designed to run the cutting-edge software of our souls? Or is it more like a hostage situation – is the body a time bomb strapped to our existence, the thing that will bring the action movie of our life to a sudden, unpredictable end?
>
> (Anderson, 2022, p. 13)

Although Anderson's questions are partly designed to entertain and amuse, we believe they reflect a widely shared perplexity. He responds to his own questions as follows:

> Well, I don't know. None of us do. This is one of the gnawing weirdnesses of being human. It is impossible to think your body; you can only really *body* your body. And so we walk around with this feeling of mild

DOI: 10.4324/9781003265047-10

alienation, this basic incoherence – a dualism that runs all the way down to the roots of Western culture.

(Anderson, 2022, p. 13)

We agree with Anderson that the mild alienation we feel toward our bodies, which undoubtedly has deep roots in our culture, cannot be resolved by means of thought, by disembodied concepts. Moreover, we believe that to "body the body" requires a process of learning, a conscious effort to attend to bodily feelings that we have been subtly taught to ignore. We have tried to show how we help therapists attend to their own bodies and those of their patients with the supervision model we outlined in the last chapter.

It strikes us that another reason that an embodied psychoanalysis was slow to gain prominence was that Western science tended to view the body in terms of biology, physics and energy. As we have already suggested (see Chapter 1), Wilhelm Reich was the first analyst to show that humans talk not only with words but with their whole bodies. As he became increasingly convinced about the centrality of bodily experience, he saw no alternative but to conceive of bodily experience as bio-energetic and biophysical. This is clearly expressed in the last part of his book, *Character Analysis* (1933/49), which he titled "*From Psychoanalysis to Orgone Biophysics*." Consequently, many who were inspired by Reich concluded that body-focused treatment had to be grounded in non-psychoanalytic modalities based on neurobiology or neuro-energy.

As we see it, the body could not be conceptualized in psychological terms before the groundbreaking philosophical work of Maurice Merleau-Ponty. Until then, the choice had been between a disembodied psychoanalysis or non-psychoanalytic therapies that viewed the body in terms of biology and/ or physics.

We also suspect that Freud's own theory may have inadvertently prevented his followers from developing ways to teach analysts to attend to their bodies. It seems that his one-person drive theory – a reflection of the energy-discharge science of his time – was increasingly found to be incompatible with contemporary science and relational theories. As a result, many analysts turned away from the body entirely. Heinz Kohut (1959), for example, strenuously objected to Franz Alexander's and French's (1946) efforts to explain various medical syndromes in depth-psychological terms by means of "the drives." In his effort to eliminate traces of what he called "psychobiology," (Kohut, 1959) referred to empathy as the definer of a field of "pure psychology."

Nevertheless, Kohut's interest in the body was evident throughout his writings; references to "body-self" pepper his work. As early as 1971, in *The Analysis of the Self*, he explained that the fragmentation common in narcissistic personality disorders was often manifested in a preoccupation with and worry about single body parts. This, he said, came to "replace the experience of a total mind-body-self."

Moreover, for Kohut, the experience of twinship, which he identified along with mirroring and idealization as a vital self-object experience, involves a sense of humans as embodied. For example, he writes:

> The mere presence of people in a child's surroundings – their voices and body odors, the emotions they express, the noises they produce as they engage in human activities, the specific aroma of the foods they prepare and eat – creates a security in the child, a sense of belonging and participating, that cannot be explained in terms of mirroring or merger with ideals.
>
> (Kohut, 1984, p. 200)

Yet, as of the time of his death, Kohut had not called attention to the fact that all psychological phenomena are embodied, nor that all that is experienced in the analytic setting is felt in the bodies of analysts as well as patients.

The skin problem

While there is no more powerful way to express a sense of human belonging than through touch, it was only in the last presentation he gave at Berkeley, shortly before he died, that Kohut actually mentioned touch. In his presentation, Kohut noted that "people with very serious self-disturbances, who cannot possibly benefit from interpretations . . . do need an empathic understanding on the closest level that we can muster" (p. 535). He seems to have suggested that touch provides that level by admitting that he had offered an "extremely vulnerable" patient two fingers to hold. Then he offered this explanation for what took place:

> She took a hold of them (my fingers) and I immediately made a genetic interpretation to myself. It was the toothless gums of a very young child clamping down on an empty nipple. That was the way it felt. I didn't say anything. I don't know whether it was right. But I reacted to it even there, to myself, as an analyst.
>
> (Kohut/Ornstein, 1981/1991, p. 535)

Clearly Kohut had grave misgivings about allowing his patient to touch even two of his fingers, so grave that he could not allow the skin-to-skin contact between him and his patient to be enough in itself. He felt compelled to imagine his patient at her mother's empty breast. The taboo against touch that has haunted psychoanalysis through the years undoubtedly had a powerful effect on him.

Much has been written about the negative consequences of touch between patients and analysts – especially when that touch has had sexual meanings. Analysts fearful of being charged with sexually violating their patients have avoided even the most benign forms of nonsexual touch at all cost. With the rise of the #metoo movement in the United States and other countries around the world, fears about the sexual connotations of touch have reinforced the long-standing touch taboo.

> Aron and Starr (2013) noted that for more than 100 years discussions about the history of touch in the consulting room usually began with Freud's account of touching his patients' heads to aid in memory retrieval during the course of hypnosis. However, in their view, "the talking cure" emerged from Freud's involvement in and eventual rejection of the standard treatment of hysteria, which included stimulating women's genitals by manual and vibratory massage, hydrotherapy, or electrotherapy to bring them to orgasm. It is little wonder that, over time, the psychoanalytic standards of neutrality, anonymity and non-gratification came to be understood as incompatible with any form of touch! One result was that psychotherapies using touch in one form or another were considered "not psychoanalytic." In fact, touch was one of the elements that came to define the binary between psychoanalysis and psychotherapy throughout the 20th century.
>
> (Aron and Starr, 2013)

Until very recently, most psychoanalytic conference presentations and journal articles failed to mention the claps on the shoulders, hugs, held hands and other forms of touch that pervade analyses. Guntrip's famous article comparing his analyses with Fairbairn and Winnicott is a rare exception. After describing how Winnicott held out his hand for a friendly handshake at the end of sessions, he writes:

> As I was finally leaving Fairbairn after the last session, I suddenly realized that in all that long period we had never once shaken hands, and he was letting me leave without that friendly gesture. I put out my hand and at once he took it, and I suddenly saw a few tears trickle down his face. I saw the warm heart of this man with a fine mind and a shy nature.
>
> (Guntrip, 1996, 744)

Why was this handshake so transformative? Consider these lines by William Cornell: "The human hand. The human reach. The human touch. From the moment of birth, we discover ourselves in and through the hands of others, in our vitality and vulnerability" (2015, p. 47). In fact, as the research of Rene Spitz (1945) confirmed, infants deprived of human touch not only fail to develop a coherent sense of self, they become subject to what he called "anaclitic depression" or "hospitalism," and suffer irreparable psychosomatic damage. Many infants waste away. While analysts must, on some level, have understood the value of touch for neglected and emotionally deprived patients, it is not something that they have spoken about. A notable exception is Edward Novak's (2023) book, *Physical Touch in Psychoanalytic Psychotherapy*.

In the hope of contributing to a more nuanced psychoanalytic perspective on touch, we offer the concept of "skinship," which we believe is a way of adding embodiment to Kohut's notion of "twinship" as feeling human among other human beings. We conceive of "skinship" in terms of experiences that are embodied and mutually shared by means of nonsexual touch. Skinship, then, may be thought of as *the experience of freedom shared by patients and therapists to touch (or not to touch) one another in nonsexual ways*. It is often conveyed through the forms of touch that frequently occur within psychoanalytic encounters but are so often omitted from clinical writings. We now offer two brief clinical examples to illustrate these ideas.

Doris and Tina

Seated in the chair facing mine, Tina, a Hispanic woman in her late 40s, was clearly ill at ease in her first meeting with me. She held her hugely fat body in a tense unmoving way, her hands gripping the arms of the chair. After a few minutes, she said that she felt very uncomfortable and would try sitting on a small couch that was located much farther away from my chair. At once, Tina seemed to relax and to move her body more freely, using the large gestures I have come to recognize as typically hers.

Explaining her reason for seeking analysis, she said that since her elderly father was suffering from what was likely a fatal illness, it seemed urgent that she deal with his sexual molestation of her that occurred when she was 12 years old. After becoming quite promiscuous during adolescence, her increasing weight gain had resulted in abstinence from sex. Although she now lived with a boyfriend, their sexual relationship had all but ended years earlier. We came to understand her weight gain in terms of her dread of re-experiencing the feelings of mortification and betrayal that she experienced during sexual contact with her father. We imagined that she had unconsciously padded herself with fat as protection against even benign forms of touch that often held sexual meanings for her. She was convinced that "no one really wants to touch a very fat person."

Since she declared herself ready to end the episodes of "sugar binging" (her words for consuming vast amounts of candy and ice cream in a single sitting) that had begun immediately after the molestation by her father, we spent a number of sessions closely examining them. At the end of one session, she suddenly announced, "I think I eat to recapture the sweetness of my relationship with my father. It ended when he molested me." She then revealed that although she felt close to her mother, they had never shared the hugs and tender caresses that made her contact with her father "sweet." In recent years, her mother seemed ashamed and even physically revolted by Tina's fatness. She continually urged her to diet and exercise.

As time went by, Tina trusted me with more and more intimate details of her early life, her relationships with friends, as well as her present professional conflicts. After about a year and a half, Tina decided to try to move back to the chair close to mine. I was delighted when she announced that the couch was "too far away from you."

A turning point in our relationship occurred during a session shortly after her father died. Clearly grief-stricken, Tina had fallen silent, her vacant eyes were downcast and she slumped in her seat. Although we had never touched before, I felt a strong urge to take her hand. Concerned that she would feel intruded upon, I simply extended my hand toward her. She lifted her hand and turned her palm upward. I turned my hand so that our palms met as we both leaned toward each other. We stayed like this for some minutes until Tina began to weep. Tears rolled down my cheeks as well.

Talking about this moment during our next meeting, Tina said that in addition to crying over the loss of her father, she was also weeping for the poignant message my touch conveyed to her: unlike her mother, I must not have found her fat repulsive. The newfound "sweetness" in our relationship, which now involves hugs at the end of our sessions, seems to have led to some positive changes in Tina's life. Although she is still very much overweight, she is now working out weekly with a personal trainer and has resumed sexual relations with her boyfriend.

Doris and Grace

If touching was an important element in my relationship with Tina, not touching was equally important in my relationship with Grace, an attractive and successful businesswoman. Having been divorced after a ten-year marriage, she had recently ended a relationship with another man.

Grace confessed that her world was populated with people who had sought her companionship. Characterizing herself as "passive," she said that she had never approached anyone for friendship or romance – others always initiated the contacts. Since she wondered if she had "truly loved" anyone, I was very surprised when, after only a few months of sessions, Grace told me that she liked me very much. "I really look forward to coming to see you. It's the first time I've ever felt this way about anyone," she said.

Grace's experience of verbalizing positive feeling for me seems to have awakened her to a world of feelings that had largely been missing in her early life. Her parents were hardworking immigrants who had rarely given verbal expression to feelings of any kind. "I was a good girl," she said, "and I tried to behave in ways that made them happy." Because they seemed clearly uncomfortable when Grace expressed feelings, particularly strongly negative or positive ones, she had avoided doing so.

Like a child enjoying her new ability to skip rope or ride a bike, Grace frequently announced her freshly discovered feelings with great pride. For example, she recognized that she was angry with her brother and wished that he would act on his frequent threats to end his life. She felt strongly attracted to a man she met at her gym. "Could I be falling in love?" she asked me with undisguised delight.

From our first meeting on, I had never felt the slightest inclination to touch Grace. Nor had she shown any desire to touch me. It's as if our bodies had not called to one another's for physical contact. I was very puzzled about the lack of physical connectedness of any kind between us until she mentioned in an offhand way that she missed the back rubs that were always given at the dining room table in her family's home. "Back rubs?" I asked. Grace explained that very often a member of the family would rub the back of everyone seated at the table and that not a word about it was ever spoken. In response to my inquiries, she noted that everyone in her family was physically affectionate. Although kisses and hugs and back rubs were routinely exchanged, no words had ever accompanied these demonstrations of loving connectedness.

We then understood that the physical manifestation of feelings was not enough for Grace. She had needed an exchange of words about the feelings that had been demonstrated physically in order to experience her feelings as authentically hers. By using words and not touch, I had allowed Grace to experience her feelings as hers for the first time.

Touch figured importantly in my relationships with Tina and Grace, as it does in many encounters between patients and therapists – especially when sexual desire becomes prominent. Then the decision to touch or not touch can powerfully affect the therapeutic outcome. But the meanings associated with touching or not touching may be quite subtle and difficult to identify. Many therapeutic issues come into play. Should the desire to touch be spoken about? When? How? What sexual meanings might touch convey? How do the cultural backgrounds of the analytic couple influence whether and how they may touch?

Since the beginning of the COVID pandemic, many therapeutic relationships have been conducted on screens. Without the possibility for touch, it may be easy to ignore the feelings associated with the desire for skin-to-skin contact. But that does not necessarily mean that they are absent. We believe that there is much to gain from attending to the ways in which our bodies talk about skinship with our patients – even if they are not within reach.

Transcending the body

In a qualitative research study that investigates how psychotherapists become aware of and make sense of their embodied reactions, or "somatic countertransference," Zeyneb Catay (Güçlü & Çatay, in press) examined reasons for the neglect of the body among psychotherapists. She mentioned, for example, that therapists found it easier to privilege "the mind," as if the mind and body were in conflict such that focus on one leads to the neglect of the other. We imagine that "mind" in this context means the verbal aspects of the therapeutic exchange.

She also found that therapists avoided focusing on their bodies for fear of "losing control, not knowing and losing face." She cited literature suggesting that therapists may close off perception of their bodies to avoid intense affective experiences that could reveal things about themselves that they were not prepared to know.

However, there may well be an even more powerful reason for the neglect of embodiment in psychoanalysis; a longing to transcend the bodily bases of experience has pervaded our world from time immemorial. Efforts to transcend the body are to be found in the use of psychedelic substances such as LSD and in certain spiritual practices involving either bodily stillness or repetitive movements.

What has led to this longing to escape the limitations imposed by our bodily nature? We do not pretend to know the answer to this question, but we can think of several possible explanations. Not only are bodies subject to immense pain and suffering, but they die. The inevitability of our own death and that of our loved ones fills us with terror. Many psychologists have studied the universal tendency to deny death (e.g., Becker, 1974). It is not only the end of our own going on being that we dread but, as Kohut (1984) has observed, even more devastating is the knowledge that we must relinquish our connections to others. It is little wonder that so many religions offer their adherents hope of some sort of an afterlife in which loved ones meet again.

Another reason that we may wish to transcend bodily experience is that the differences in human embodiment often create great challenges for us. Bodies not only differ with respect to sex, race and skin color, they also reflect differences in class, culture and sexual orientation. As we have seen in Chapter 6, these differences may give rise to us-them conflicts, some involving horrible destructiveness. The more analysts open themselves to their bodily reactions to patients, the more they are likely to notice their feelings about the patient's physicality – their beauty, weight, racial characteristics, etc. Perhaps sitting behind patients as they recline on a couch, as Freud did, kept traditional analysts from attending to their bodily reactions to their patients.

Those of us who choose to engage in a truly embodied psychoanalytic practice must be willing to tolerate all the complicated, and at times, painful feelings generated by the intermingling of *I, you, we* and **world.** While we cannot minimize the difficulties this entails, the rewards, we believe, could not be greater.

References

Alexander, F., & French, T. M. (1946). *Psychoanalytic therapy*. New York: Ronald Press.
Anderson, S. (2022). I've always struggled with mt weight. Losing it didn't mean winning. *New York Times Magazine*, 11 May, pp. 10–15. https://www.nytimes.com›weight-loss-pandemic

Aron, L., & Starr, K. (2013). *A psychotherapy for the people: Toward a progressive psychoanalysis*. New York & London: Routledge.

Becker, E. (1974). *The denial of death*. New York: Simon and Schuster.

Brothers, D., & Sletvold, J. (2022). Talking bodies: A new vision of psychoanalysis. *Psychoanalytic Inquiry, 42*(4), 289–302. https://doi.org/10.1080/07351690.2022.2059292

Cornell, W. (2015). *Somatic experience in psychoanalysis and psychotherapy in the expressive language of the living*. New York and London: Routledge.

Güçlü, A., & Çatay, Z. (in press). *Hearing, feeling, sensing: How do somatic countertransference reactions enter into the field of meaning making*.

Guntrip, H. (1996). My experience of analysis with fairbairn and winnicott: How complete a result does therapy achieve? *International Journal of Psychoanalysis, 77*, 739–754.

Kohut, H. (1959). Introspection, empathy, and psychoanalysis – An examination of the relationship between mode of observation and theory. *Journal of the American. Psychoanalytic Association, 7*, 459–483.

Kohut, H. (1984). *How does analysis cure?* Chicago, IL: University of Chicago Press. http://dx.doi.org/10.7208/chicago/9780226006147.001.0001

Kohut, H., & Ornstein, P. (1991). *The search for the self: selected writings of Heinz Kohut 1978–1981* (Vol. 4). New York and London, England: Routledge.

Novak, E. T. (2023). *Physical touch in psychoanalytic psychotherapy*. London, England and New York: Routledge.

Spitz, R. (1945). Anaclitic depression: An Inquiry into the genesis of psychiatric conditions in early childhood, II. *The Psychoanalytic Study of the Child, 2*(1), 313–342.

Coda

We end our book with some ideas we hope you will want to take with you:

- Psychoanalytic dialogues are conducted by talking bodies – sometimes with words and sometimes without them.
- Bodies talk about *I, you, we* and **world.**
- The flow of attention among *I, you, we* and *world* for one person complexly intermingles with the *I-you-we-world* flow for that person's relational partners.
- Traumatic experiences tend to slow or freeze the flow of *I, you, we* and *world* such that only one component comes to the foreground while the others slip into the background. This dissociative activity reduces the complexity and sensed uncertainty of lived experience.
- Because we all live in a traumatized and traumatizing world, the flow of *I-you-we-world* is never completely fluid.
- Many constitutional factors, including subtle neurological conditions such as ADHD and high-functioning autism, also interfere with the *I-you-we-world* flow.
- The creation of binaries is another way in which experience is simplified in the aftermath of trauma. Binaries constrict *world* and limit how *I, you* and *we* interact with the *world*. We are all vulnerable to the *us-them* binary.
- Psychoanalytic healing involves increasing the fluidity of the *I-you-we-world* flow for patients and analysts. This tends to be accomplished by means of enhancing the embodied *we*-connectedness of the analytic partners.
- It is possible to learn how to increase one's awareness of how bodies talk in psychoanalytic relationships. Such learning benefits from embodied supervision.

The patient's perception
of the analyst

In this book we have maintained that neither the analyst's perception of the patient nor the patient's perception of the analyst is sufficient to describe the analytic process. We have advanced the idea of "talking bodies" to capture the embodied reciprocity of the clinical exchange. However, some of our fellow analysts have taken steps to remedy the traditional view that what mattered was the analyst's perception of the patient. According to Lewis Aron (1991): "Patients seek to connect to their analysts, to know them, to probe beneath their professional façade" (p. 29).

In what follows, we first present the views of analysts who have argued that the patient's view of the analyst has been neglected. Then we give some examples of work in which the patient's experience of the analyst is featured. We conclude by providing accounts by two of Freud's patient's about their experience of Freud's bodily presence, and an account by Erich Fromm's biographer of his experience of Fromm.

In *The Patient's Experience of the Analyst's Subjectivity*, Lewis Aron (1991) suggests that the exploration of the patient's experience of the analyst represents an underestimated aspect of psychoanalysis, and that it ought to be an essential part of an explication of the therapeutic relationship.

> We need to recognize that our own self-awareness is limited and that we are not in a position to judge the accuracy of our patient's perceptions of us. Thus, the idea that we might "validate" or "confirm" our patients' perceptions of us is presumptuous.
>
> (p. 49)

Aron (1991) recounts that when presenting his ideas to collogues and students, he was struck by an overwhelming tendency on the part of the listeners to focus the discussion on the analyst's self-revelations, rather than the patient's experience of the analyst. Aron suggests the reason that analytic audiences prefer to focus on self-disclosure, namely, that patients who seek to "know" their analysts raise profound anxieties for analysts who both long to be known and feel tempted to hide.

Steven Kuchuck (2021) has recently argued that a lack of interest in the patients' perceptions of their analysts still exists, even among relational analysts. In line with Aron, he speculates that many of us are drawn to the psychoanalytic profession, in part as an opportunity to hide our personhood, for the sake of rescuing first our parents, and now our patients.

> When we theorize, present and write, a natural extension of this dynamic emerges in an almost exclusive focus on the patient's psychology rather than our own. . . . A healthy therapist treating an ill patient. . . . It's a split born of early wounds, training mandates, our professional ego ideal and cultural pressures that reinforce the notion of the powerful, "fully analyzed" clinician.
>
> (p. 30–31)

Sandberg and Beebe (2020) have recently reported on a remarkable study of a patient's perception of the therapist. Sandberg's patient Sandra had developed chronic gaze aversion. After "all interpretative efforts focused on understanding the meaning of her gaze aversion fell flat" (p. 479), Sandberg invited Beebe to do video feedback with Sandra. Beebe videotaped herself with Sandra, and afterward they looked at the video of Beebe together. Beebe, discussing the first video, commented on how sad her own face looked. Sandra then responded:

> You put yourself in my shoes. You allow me to be sad, a new experience. You are not angry with me. You give me the sense of existing in front of you. . . . You made me live with my sadness.

Beebe: Is it different with Dr. Sandberg?
Sandra: *I don't see his face.* It was important to allow me to watch you. I saw you have concern, empathy. (p. 485)

According to Sandberg, it was shocking for Sandra to experience Beebe's face as different from her mother's. It was liberating but also terrifying. She had a recognition of her mother's face as cruel and full of hatred. She had held on to the idea that her mother was hitting her to put her on the right track. Beebe concluded that Sandra had to see an empathic face to recognize her own sadness; "A year later she told me she had not looked directly at anyone's face since she was about 12 years old" (485).

Sandberg and Beebe state that their work would not be considered psychoanalytic in a traditional sense, but assert that "the video feedback was psychoanalytically informed and crucial in catalyzing a deepening analytic experience for the patient and stimulating psychic growth" (497).

The importance of the patient's perception of the therapist is also illustrated in a study conducted by Bernhardt, Nissen-Lie & Råbu (2020). They interviewed 16 therapists who worked within the public mental health system in Norway and who were judged by their clinic managers as likely to establish constructive psychotherapy processes with patients. The case reported in this study was selected because it illustrated how the therapist's personal way of being might contribute to therapeutic change. The way this therapist used his bodily, nonverbal presence distinguished him from the other therapists in this research project.

Referring to his own personal therapy one therapist said:

> Through the attention, intimacy, and authenticity my therapist showed me, I became more real in a way. I became important. I could easily have gone through years of therapy just talking, being analyzed, or being subject to behavioral therapy, but I think his way of being bodily present connected with me on another level – it allowed me to develop from just being someone that adjusts and accommodates to what other people need.
>
> (p. 6)

With respect to the case reported in this research project, the therapist said: "I never really knew how to proceed. But I just said to myself that I had to endure these feelings of insecurity in order for the process to move further" (p. 7). The patient described her relationship with the therapist as follows:

> I feel we have chemistry – we are a good match, which means I can be myself with him. I can use my irony and humor and – maybe he thinks I am a little crazy sometimes, he laughs, but he always brings me back to the "heart of the matter."
>
> (p. 7)

The researchers concluded that it seems important to reach a state of "emotional togetherness" that seems to depend as much upon the patient's perceptions of the therapist as on the therapist's perceptions of the patient.

The patient's perception of the embodied presence of the analyst might have been part of psychoanalysis and psychotherapy from it very inception. To illustrate this perspective, we recount how the Wolf-Man and Hilda Doolittle experienced their meeting with Freud.

The Wolf-Man's experience of Freud

The Wolf-Man met Freud for the first time in 1910 after having consulted with several of the foremost psychiatrists and neurologists of the time. The Wolf-Man describes his first meeting with Freud in *My Recollections of Sigmund Freud* (Gardiner, 1973) as follows:

> Freud's appearance was such as to win my confidence immediately. He was then in his middle fifties and seemed to enjoy the best of health. He was a medium height and figure. In his rather long face, framed by

a closely clipped, already greying beard, the most impressive feature was his intelligent dark eyes, which looked at me penetratingly but without causing me the slightest feeling of discomfort. . . . Freud's whole attitude, and the way in which he listened to me, differentiated him strikingly from his famous colleagues whom I had hitherto known and in whom I had found such a lack of deeper psychological understanding. . . . After the first few hours with Freud, I felt that I had at last found what I had so long been seeking.

(Gardiner, 1973, p. 155)

After criticizing "classical" psychiatry for drawing too sharp a distinction between what is healthy and sick, the Wolf-Man writes: "Although Freud certainly did not underestimate the neurotic in his patients, he attempted always to support and strengthen the kernel of health, separated from the chaff of neuroses" (Gardiner, 1973, p. 156).

The Wolf-Man's description of his experience of analysis with Freud resonates more with contemporary relational and intersubjective views than with many accounts of classical analysis. "I can . . . say that in my analysis with Freud I felt myself less as a patient than as a co-worker, the younger comrade of an experienced explorer setting out to study a new, recently discovered land" (Gardiner, 1973, p. 158).

Not only did Freud's appearance have a great impact on him, so did the consulting room. The Wolf-Man writes:

There was always a feeling of sacred peace and quiet here. The rooms themselves must have been a surprise to any patient, for they in no way reminded one of a doctor's office but rather of an archaeologist's study. . . . Everything here contributed to one's feeling of leaving the haste of modern life behind, of being sheltered from one's daily cares.

(Gardiner, 1973, p. 157)

The Wolf-Man's high estimation of Freud lasted through his whole treatment; he never expressed any criticism or disagreement with Freud. However, this did not prevent the Wolf-Man from developing an understanding of the reasons for his emotional suffering that differed sharply from Freud's own hypothesis. Freud writes that the Wolf-Man at first seems to have been a very good-natured, tractable and even quiet child. But when his parents came back from their summer holiday, they found him transformed. He had become discontented, irritable and violent. This happened during the summer an English governess was with them. She turned out to be an eccentric and quarrelsome person who was addicted to alcohol. The boy's mother was therefore inclined to ascribe the alteration in his character to the influence of the Englishwoman. His grandmother, who had spent the summer with the children, was of the opinion that the boy's irritability had been provoked by the dissensions between the Englishwoman and the Wolf-Man's nurse. The little boy had openly taken the side of his beloved "Nanya" and let the governess see his hatred. "However it may have been, the Englishwoman was sent away soon after the parents' return, without there being any consequent change in the child's unbearable behavior" (Gardiner, 1973, pp. 178–179).

Freud formulates what he refers to as "the riddles for which the analysis had to find a solution. What was the origin of the sudden change in the boy's character?" (Gardiner, 1973, pp. 181). Freud starts his answer by stating that it is easy to understand that the first suspicion fell upon the English governess, for the change in the boy made its appearance while she was there. Freud however reached another explanation when the patient suddenly called to mind that, when he was still very small his sister had seduced him into sexual practices; she "had taken hold of his penis and played with it" (Gardiner, 1973, p. 183).

Freud stresses that the Wolf-Man's "seduction by his sister was certainly not a phantasy" (Gardiner, 1973, p. 183). Freud never abandoned his sexual abuse/seduction theory, but combined it with his newly developed theory of infantile sexuality.

According to Freud, the Wolf-Man was three-and-one-quarter years old at the time his sister began her seductions, and it happened in the spring of the year the English governess arrived. When his parents returned in the autumn, they found him fundamentally altered. Freud concludes: "It is very natural, then, to connect this transformation with the awakening of his sexual activity that had meanwhile taken place" (Gardiner, 1973, p. 187).

Freud goes on to state that it is possible to divide the Wolf-Man's childhood into two phases: a first phase of naughtiness and perversity from his seduction at the age of three and a quarter up to his fourth birthday, and a longer subsequent phase in which the signs of neurosis predominated. "But the event which makes this division was not an external trauma, but a dream, from which he awoke in a state of anxiety" (Gardiner, 1973, p. 192). According to Freud, the Wolf-Man dreamt that it was night and that he was lying in bed. Suddenly the window opened, and he was terrified to see that some white wolves were sitting on the big walnut tree in front of the window. There were six or seven of them. This was his first anxiety dream, and he was three, four or at most five years old at the time.

Freud begins his interpretation by stating that the dream relates to an occurrence that really took place and was not merely imagined, and then adds that he is afraid his interpretation will cause the reader to abandon him.

> What sprang into activity that night out of the chaos of the dreamer's unconscious memory-traces was the picture of copulation between his parent's, copulation in circumstances which were not entirely usual and were especially favorable for observation. Thus in the first place the child's age at the date of the observation was established as being about one and

a half years. . . . When he woke up, he witnessed a coitus a tergo . . . he was able to see his mother's genitals as well as his father's organ; and he understood the process as well as its significance.

(Gardiner, 1973, pp. 199–200)

The Wolf-Man had witnessed what Freud came to regard as the primal scene at an age of one and a half years. Freud summarizes his theoretical understanding as follows:

The steps in the transformation of the material – primal scene – wolf dream – fairy tale of The Seven Little Goats – are a reflection of the progress of the dreamer's thought during the construction of the dream: longing for sexual satisfaction from his father – realization that castration is a necessary condition of it – fear of his father. It is only at this point, I think, that we can regard the anxiety-dream of this four-year-old boy as being exhaustively explained.

(Gardiner, 1973, p. 205)

Freud's explanation of the Wolf-Man's childhood problems is entirely in keeping with the theory he had been developing the foregoing 10–15 years. Soon after the publication (with Breuer) of Studies on Hysteria (1893/95), he abandoned the general trauma theory of hysteria/neurosis, first in favor of the theory of sexual abuse/seduction, and then in terms of his theory of infantile sexual drives (Sletvold, 2016). In his explanation of the Wolf-Man's "infantile neurosis," Freud combines his second and third theory. He was now convinced that the cause of neurosis is sexual in nature. He writes:

Unless these sexual traumas of childhood were taken into account it was impossible either to elucidate the symptoms . . . or to prevent their recurrence. In this way the unique significance of sexual experiences in the aetiology of the psychoneuroses seemed to be established beyond doubt; and this fact remains to this day one of the corner-stones of my theory.

(1906 [1905]), p. 273)

Having reached this conviction, it was impossible for Freud to accept that the Wolf-Man's childhood emotional problems could have resulted from being left in the hands of the English governess during his parents' several months of absence.

The Wolf-Man himself, however, understood his problems very differently from Freud. He wrote:

I have been told also that in my early childhood I was a quiet, almost phlegmatic child, but that my character changed completely after the arrival of the English governess, Miss Oven. Although she was with us only a few months, I became a very nervous, irritable child, subject to severe temper tantrums.

Soon after Miss Oven came to us, my parents left home to travel abroad, leaving my sister Anna and me in the care of my Nanya and Miss Oven. Anna was two and a half years older than I, and Miss Oven was evidently engaged more for her than for me. My parents had left the supervision of both Miss Oven and my Nanya to our maternal grandmother, who unfortunately did not really assume this responsibility. Although she was aware of Miss Oven's harmful influence on me, she did not dare to dismiss her, and kept waiting for the return of our parents. This return was delayed over and over again, so that Miss Oven, who was either a severe psychopath or often under the influence of alcohol, continued her mischief for several month.

It is difficult to know what went on. I can remember, and our grandmother confirmed this, that angry quarrels broke out between my Nanya and me on the one side and Miss Oven on the other. Evidently Miss Oven kept teasing me, and knew how to arouse my fury, which must have given her some sort of sadistic satisfaction.

(Gardiner, 1973, pp. 19–21)

We see that Freud and the Wolf-Man are in agreement about what seems to be the most obvious reason for the Wolf-man's "infantile neurosis," namely that his parents left him for several months to be taken care of by a governess the Wolf-Man describes as a psychopathic alcoholic. Freud however dismisses this explanation in favor of an explanation based on his theory of infantile sexuality and sexual trauma (seduction).

There are no signs that the Wolf-Man raised any objections to Freud's suggestions during the analysis, and he states his own view in his memoirs without in any way indicating that this view differs from Freud's. The Wolf-Man kept his deep appreciation of Freud unshackled.

Hilda Doolittle's experience of Freud

Hilda Doolittle, an outstanding poet, was born in Pennsylvania in 1886, and died in Switzerland in 1961. She started her analysis with Freud on March 1, 1933, after a recommendation by Hanns Sachs. In "Writing on the Wall," written in the autumn of 1944, Doolittle describes her first meeting with Freud in the following way.

The first impression of all takes me back to the beginning, to my first session with the Professor. Paula has opened the door (though I did not then know that the pretty little Viennese maid was called Paula). . . . She has shown me into the waiting room with the lace curtains at the window, with framed photographs of celebrities, some known personally to me;

Dr. Havelock Ellis and Dr. Hanns Sachs gaze at me, familiar but a little distorted in their frames under the reflecting glass. . . . I wait in this room. I know that Prof. Dr. Sigmund Freud will open the door which faces me. Although I know this and have been preparing for some months for this ordeal. I am, nonetheless, taken aback, surprised, shocked even, when the door opens. It seems to me, after my time of waiting, that he appears too suddenly.

Automatically, I walk through the door. It closes. Sigmund Freud does not speak. He is waiting for me to say something. I cannot speak. I look around the room. A lover of Greek art, I am automatically taking stock of the rooms content. . . . Pricelessly lovely objects are placed here. . . . But all this is a feeling, an atmosphere – something that I realize or perceive, but do not actually put into words or thoughts. I could not have said this even if I had, at that moment, realized it.

(Doolittle, 2012, p. 95–96)

I should have thought the Door-Keeper, at home beyond the threshold, might have greeted the shivering soul. Not so, the Professor. . . . But waiting and finding that I would not or could not speak, he uttered. What he said – and I thought a little sadly – was, "You are the only person who has ever come into this room and looked at the things in the room before looking at me."

But worse was to come. A little lion-like creature came padding toward me – a lioness, as it happened. She had emerged from the inner sanctum or manifested from under or behind the couch; anyhow, she continued her course across the carpet. Embarrassed, shy, overwhelmed, I bend down to greet this creature. But the Professor says, "Do not touch her – she snaps – she is very difficult with strangers." Strangers? Is the Soul crossing the threshold a stranger . . . to the Door-Keeper? It appears so. But, though no accredited dog-lover, I like dogs and they oddly and sometimes unexpectedly "take" to me. If this is an exception, I am ready to take the risk. Unintimidated but distressed by the Professor's somewhat forbidding manner, I not only continue my gesture toward the chow, but crouch on the floor so that she can snap better if she wants to. Yofi – her name is Yofi – snuggles her nose into my hand and nuzzles her head, in delicate sympathy, against my shoulder.

So again I can say the Professor was not always right. That is, yes, he was always right in his judgments, but my form of rightness, my intuition, sometimes functioned by the split-second. . . . My intuition challenges the Professor, though not in words. That intuition cannot really be translated unto words, but if it could be it would go, roughly, something like this: "Why should I look at you? You are contained in the things you love, and if you accuse me of looking at the things in the room before looking at you, well, I will go on looking at the things in the room. One of them is this little golden dog. She snaps, does she? You call me a stranger, do you? Well, I will show you two things: one, I am now no longer one. And moreover I never was a stranger to this little golden Yofi."

The wordless challenge goes on, "You are a very great man. I am overwhelmed with embarrassment, I am shy and frightened and gauche as an over-grown school-girl. But listen. You are a man. Yofi is a dog. I am a woman. If this dog and this woman "take" to one another, it will prove that beyond your caustic implied criticism – if criticism it is – there is another region of cause and effect, another region of question and answer." Undoubtedly, the Professor took an important clue from the first reaction of a new analysand or patient. I was, as it happened, not prepared for this. It would have been worse for me if I had been.

(Doolittle, 2012, p. 125–129)

What is striking about Doolittle's story is how much she experienced during the first seconds of her meeting with Freud. She formed strong impressions of Freud and herself, but she stresses that it was only later that she was able to put these impressions into words.

It is also worth noting that Doolittle herself downplays the verbal content of her analysis with Freud: "I cannot classify the living content of our talks together by recounting them in a logical or textbook manner. It was, as he said of my grandfather, 'an atmosphere'" (Doolittle, 2012, p. 137).

We believe that the the Wolf-Man's and Hilda Doolittle's descriptions of meeting Freud suggest that these patients "analyzed" Freud as much as he analyzed them. It seems that this "mutual analysis" begins in the very first seconds of the first meeting, if not before.

Rainer Funk's experience of Eric Fromm

We end this appendix with a review of Rainer Funk's (2019) perceptions of Eric Fromm. Funk met Eric Fromm not as a patient but as a professional with a strong interest in his theories. He introduces Fromm under the headings "*Face to face*" and "*This is you*":

Fromm looked at me in such a straightforward way that my attempts at polite conversation ceased abruptly and any superficial courtesies became unnecessary . . . Somehow Fromm's eyes, encircled by wrinkles and scrutinizing me intently, managed to initiate a conversation that allayed my anxieties and made it possible for me to concentrate intently. . . .

Through his interest and questions, Fromm wanted to get in touch with my inner world. . . . To do so, he used eye contact. . . . Naturally, at the time I was incapable of fully comprehending this. What I did sense, however, was that Fromm had a special way of approaching me: it had a great deal to do with his gaze, which one could hardly evade. The pupils of his blue, myopic eyes behind the rimless eyeglasses appeared to be diminished in size, causing his look to seem almost penetrating. His gaze corresponded to his way of being interested in my inner life, my soul. . . . Despite the directness and bluntness . . . I did not at all feel interrogated, cornered, judged, unmasked, or exposed. I quickly sensed that he was dealing with me in a pleasant way, with understanding and warmheartedness, and that I had no inclination to justify or conceal myself. . . .

This type of human encounter was an entirely new experience for me: this way of conversing, of being with the other, of venturing into that world of feelings and passions at work behind our thinking. . . . Initiated by Fromm, this experience signaled the beginning of a new intellectual approach for me. . . .

During our first personal encounter I had the impression that the arguments with which I had intended to dispute Fromm's humanism were obtuse and beside the point. With my intellectual weapons, that is, logical arguments, I had wanted to challenge, not concede, I had wanted to be right, not rational. While I had sought confrontation, Fromm offered a face-to-face encounter. The way he approached me was completely disarming. . . . But it wasn't actually the topics under discussion that caused me to notice the effects of his art of living, as interesting and entertaining as these were. It was the face-to-face encounter that Fromm made possible, regardless of the subject matter, which had clearly perceptible effects on me.

(Funk, 2019, pp. 2–9)

Like the Wolf-Man's meeting with Freud, Funk's meeting with Fromm was very positive. But we present them, not because these analysts were so highly regarded, but rather because they highlight the centrality of bodily emotional expression. And they demonstrate how such expression enhances the impact of whatever words might be spoken. We suggest that what is crucially important for those who knew Freud and Fromm, in addition to their theoretical contributions, were their bodily ways of being with others, their ways of being with *you*. In other words, we believe that how these analysts were perceived laid the foundation for whatever impact their interpretations and verbal interventions have had.

Throughout the 20th century, the focus of psychoanalytic treatment remained on the analyst's interpretation of the patient. An important exception to this was the Norwegian psychoanalyst Harald Schjelderup, generally regarded as the founder of Norwegian psychoanalysis (Sletvold, 2011; 2014). Schjelderup viewed the therapeutic action of psychoanalysis as depending more on the patient's experience than on the analyst's interpretation. In an article on the personality-changing processes of psychoanalytic treatment, he wrote, "In preference to theoretical explanations, some illustrative examples will give a clear idea of *the emotional processes in the analysis – not as interpreted by the analyst, but as experienced by the patient*" (Schjelderup, 1956, p. 51, our italics).

Classical psychoanalysis privileges words that convey reflected thought. Such words form the basis of traditional interpretation and verbal interventions. In our view, words and thoughts will always have a place in psychoanalysis and psychotherapy. However, communication between humans continually involves body-based feelings and movements. When words are used, they are carried by bodily processes that are formed prior to any conscious reflection, but which may, at times, be reflected upon later.

In this book we have argued that the patient's and the analyst's experience of one another, their embodied connectedness, is foundational. Defining psychoanalysis by formal rules such as the frequency of sessions, positions in the consulting room or specific theories and techniques is inconsistent with this view. We also believe that such a view runs counter to distinguishing psychoanalysis from psychoanalytic psychotherapy. For us, it is the quality of the emotional communication, the embodied connectedness, between analyst and patient that decides the depth of the therapeutic process.

Theories are important

The Wolf-Man's theoretical disagreement with Freud did not seem to disrupt his experience of a healing relationship. This is, however, not always the case. In the case of Dora (Freud, 1905 [1901]) it seems likely that theoretical conviction, and the attitude that came with it, disrupted Dora's hope for a healing experience. When Freud treated Dora, he had just abandoned his so-called seduction theory, a theory proposing that childhood sexual abuse was the cause of hysteria. Instead, he had developed a theory suggesting that fantasies derived from repressed sexual drives, rather than real events, caused hysteria/neurosis (Sletvold, 2016). In accordance with this new theory, Freud postulated distorted sexual excitement and childhood masturbation as the causes of Dora's illness. Freud did not consider the dysfunctional and traumatizing family situation Dora described as important for understanding her difficulties. Dora's family situation included Mrs. K., who had a sexual relationship with Dora's father, and Mr. K., who attacked her sexually. Freud however was convinced that Dora's illness was caused by childhood masturbation. Here is how Freud explained Dora's experience.

> He (Mr. K) then came back, and, instead of going out by the open door, suddenly clasped the girl to him and pressed a kiss upon her lips. This was surely just the situation to call up a distinct feeling of sexual excitement in a girl of fourteen who had never before been approached. But Dora had at that moment a feeling of disgust, tor herself free from the man, and hurried past him to the staircase and from there to the street door. . . . In this scene . . . the behaviour of this child of fourteen was already entirely

and completely hysterical. I should without question consider a person hysterical in whom an occasion for sexual excitement elicited feelings that were predominantly or exclusively unpleasurable.

(SE. vol. 7, p. 28)

I met her half-way by assuring her that in my view the occurrence of leucorrhea in young girls pointed primarily to masturbation. . . . I added that she was now on the way to finding an answer to her own question of why it was that precisely she had fallen ill – by confessing that she had masturbated, probably in childhood. Dora denied flatly that she could remember any such thing.

(SE. vol. 7, p. 75)

Much to Freud's regret, Dora decided to end the treatment – a decision which, for us, made very good sense.

We want to call attention to Freud's use of expressions like "this was surely," "entirely and completely," and "without question." The attitude of knowing the patient with certainty is, in our view, more likely to be harmful than a questionable theory in itself. In the case of Dora, Freud's theory seemed to interfere with the development of the flow of *I, you, we* and **world** between him and his patient. We strongly believe that lightly held theories and those that include the idea that patient-analyst meetings are "encounters with foreignness" greatly enhance the healing process.

References

Aron, L. (1991). The patient's experience of the analyst's subjectivity. *Psychoanalytic Dialogues, 1*(1), 29–51.

Bernhardt, Nissen-Lie., & Råbu (2020). The embodied listener: A dyadic case study of how therapist and patient reflect on the significance of the therapist's personal presence for the therapeutic change process. *Psychotherapy Research*. DOI: 10.1080/10503307.2020.1808728.

Doolittle, H. (2012/1956). *Tribute to freud*. New York: A New Directions book (First published).

Freud, S. (1905/1901/1953). Fragment of an analysis of a case of hysteria. In J. Strachey (Ed. & Trans.), *The standard edition of the complete psychological works of Sigmund Freud* (Vol. 7, pp. 1–122). London, England: The Hogarth Press.

Funk, R. (2019). *Life itself is an art – The life and work of eric fromm*. New York: Bloomsbury Academic.

Gardiner, M. (1973). *The wolf-man and Sigmund Freud*. Bungay. Suffok: Pengin Books Ltd.

Kuchuck, S. (2021). *The relational revolution in psychoanalysis and psychotherapy*. London: Confer Books.

Sandberg, L. S., & Beebe, B. (2020). A patient who does not look: A collaborative treatment with video feedback. *Psychoanalytic Dialogues, 30*, 479–498.

Schjelderup, H. (1956). Personality-changing processes of psychoanalytic treatment. *Acta Psychologica, 12*, 47–64.

Sletvold, J. (2011). The reading of emotional expression. Wilhelm reich and the history of embodied analysis. *Psychoanalytic Dialogues, 21*, 453–467.

Sletvold, J. (2014). *The embodied analyst – From Freud and reich to relationality*. London, England and New York: Routledge Taylor & Francis Group.

Sletvold, J. (2016). Freud's three theories of neurosis: Towards a contemporary theory of trauma and defence. *Psychoanalytic Dialogues, 26*, 460–475. DOI: 10.1080/10481885.1190611.

Some past and present views on embodiment

We stand on the shoulders of many others who have contributed to an embodied understanding of psychoanalysis and psychotherapy. We describe some of them in this appendix.

As early as 1890, Freud (1890/1905) attempted to establish a bodily basis for psychology and psychotherapy by suggesting a connection between affects and somatic processes. He wrote:

> The affects in the narrower sense are, it is true, characterized by a quite special connection with somatic processes; but, strictly speaking, all mental states, including those that we usually regard as "processes of thought," are to some degree "affective," and not one of them is without its physical manifestation or is incapable of modifying somatic processes.
>
> (S.E. VII, p. 288)

However, eight years later Freud concluded that he had to postpone his ambition to establish a bodily foundation for his theory and therapy. Writing to Fliess on September 22, 1898, he asserted,

> I am . . . not at all inclined to leave the psychology hanging in the air without an organic basis. But apart from this conviction I do not know how to go on, neither theoretically nor therapeutically and therefore must behave as if only the psychological were under consideration.
>
> (Masson, 1985, p. 326)

Although Freud went on to develop a theory that focused on sensitive parts of the body – oral, anal and genital – this soon resulted in a concept-based rather than body-based theory. However, in 1923 Freud (1923/1961) made a new effort to embody psychoanalysis. He wrote:

> A person's own body . . . is a place from which both external and internal perceptions may spring. It is *seen* like any other object, but to the *touch* it yields two kinds of sensations, one of which may be equivalent

to an internal perception. – *The ego [ich/I] is first and foremost a bodily ego [ich/I].*

(pp. 25–26, our italics)

The psychoanalyst who took on Freud's challenge to embody psychoanalysis was Wilhelm Reich. He suggested that:

The patient's manner, look, language, countenance, dress, handshake, etc. is vastly underestimated in terms of its analytic importance. . . . At the Innsbruck Congress [1928], Ferenczi and I, independent of one another, stressed the therapeutic importance of these formal elements.

(1933/49/72, p. 31)

In the following decades, both Reich and Ferenczi became "persona non grata" within mainstream psychoanalysis. As Reich became more and more convinced about the centrality of the body, he saw it as necessary to leave psychology and psychoanalysis in favor of biophysical and bioenergetic conceptions. He titled part three of *Character Analysis* (1933/1949/1972): *From Psychoanalysis to Orgone Biophysics.*

In hindsight this move can be understood as reflecting how difficult it has been within the western world to view the body as psychological. Rather the body had to be viewed in biophysical or neurobiological terms. Only after the work of Maurice Merleau-Ponty (1945) and neuroscientists like Antonio Damasio (1994) did it become possible to envision the body as psychological. Consequently, the psychotherapies that focused on the body conceived of themselves as neuro-energetic and neurobiological modalities.

One prominent example is *Somatic Experiencing* (SE), developed by Peter Levine (2008). Holding doctorates in both medical biophysics and psychology, Levine's work focuses on post-traumatic stress disorder (PTSD). *Waking the Tiger: Healing Trauma* (1997) is the famous self-help book that he published with Ann Frederick. It presents an approach known as somatic experiencing that is designed to help people who are struggling with psychological trauma. The book discusses inhibition and release of a form of energy. *Waking the Tiger* contains four sections – Section I: The Body as Healer; Section II: Symptoms of Trauma; Section III: Transformation and Renegotiation; and Section IV: First Aid for Trauma. Levine argues that it is through action instead of talking that people who are struggling with trauma can be helped.

Levine attributes Somatic Experiencing to an experience he had in 1969 when he treated a graduate student, Nancy, who experienced severe panic attacks. Levine started their discussion with a relaxation technique. While silently paying attention, Nancy failed to react and then unexpectedly had a massive panic attack. Levine reports that, in his mind, he suddenly saw a tiger stopped low and preparing to jump at them. He shouted, "Nancy! You are being attacked by a large tiger! See the tiger as it comes toward you! Run toward that tree! Run, Nancy, run! Climb up! Escape!"

Levine says that Nancy's legs began moving as if she was sprinting. For the first time, Nancy remembered a scary childhood experience. When she was three years old, she underwent a tonsillectomy, during which she was secured to an operating table. Since the anesthesia may only have worked partially, she felt as though she was being strangled. Levine claims that his telling her to run and escape led to her healing.

Observing Nancy, Levine concluded that Nancy's panic attacks were caused by a frozen residue of energy that had gotten stuck, not the traumatic experience itself. He notes that humans cannot effortlessly release energy from a traumatic memory because human brain structure supersedes instinct.

Experts generally have not found evidence to support Levine's findings about animal responses. For example, he contends that for animals that have completely lost the ability to move, "the sudden immobility of a highly charged nervous system compresses energy that is then 'stored' in the nervous system if not released" (1997, pp. 47–48). He suggests that when animals are able to avoid predators, however, they sprint away and shake off the residual effects of the immobility response while their bodies convulse with paroxysmal spasms.

David Levit (2018) describes SE as one of a number of non-psychoanalytic approaches to treating trauma. "These neurobiologically based models focus on the body and levels of the nervous system beneath words" (p. 586). He further states:

> The interweaving of SE into psychoanalytic treatment brings together two radically different theoretical and clinical perspectives. In contrast to psychoanalytic treatment, where we focus on narratives, fantasies, and associated emotions and meanings, SE focuses primary on body sensations, urges, emotions, motions, and images.
>
> (Levit, 2018, p. 595)

From this perspective it becomes necessary to integrate non-psychoanalytic modalities rather than seeing "body sensations, urges, emotions, motions, and images" as integral and necessary parts of the analytic process.

The research of Bessel van der Kolk, a psychiatrist, author, researcher and educator based in Boston, USA, has, since the 1970s, also been devoted to post-traumatic stress. He is the author of the widely read book, *The Body Keeps the Score*, and has published over 150 peer-reviewed scientific articles. His books include *Post-traumatic Stress Disorder* (1984), *Psychological Trauma* (1987), *Traumatic Stress* (1996, with Alexander C. McFarlane and Lars Weisæth) and *The Body Keeps the Score* (2014).

In his book, *The Body Keeps the Score*, Van der Kolk (2014) contends that traumatic stress is associated with functional and chemical changes in the emotional parts of the brain – the limbic area and brain stem. He suggests that knowing the functions of the amygdala, hippocampus and prefrontal cortex, as the primary stress responders in the brain, can provide a new therapeutic direction for PTSD management. For example, the hyperactive status of the amygdala triggers the release of stress hormones and impairs the functioning of the hippocampus, causing traumatic memories to remain vivid. In addition, the deactivation of the prefrontal cortex function, and the failure to maintain a balanced stress hormone system, causes panic, agitation, and hypervigilance responses in PTSD patients. This hyperactive aroused emotional status can be evidenced by hyperactive brain waves over the fear center of the right temporal lobe of the brain, with suppression of electric activity over the frontal area.

Van der Kolk emphasizes that pharmacotherapy is vitally important in the treatment of PTSD. Antipsychotics, anticonvulsants and tranquilizers have been widely used to improve the quality of life of PTSD patients over the past few decades. Alarmed when some patients developed morbid obesity and diabetes from the medication and some suffered from drug overdoses, he developed a much safer and natural approach by means of a self-regulation strategy. Van der Kolk suggests that medication cannot "cure" trauma; it can only mediate the disruptive behavior of the sufferers.

One of Van der Kolk's patients, a minister, suffered from traumatic memories for many years after returning home from Vietnam. Van der Kolk suggested that yoga might help him regain his sense of control and bodily pleasure. A subsequent experimental study showed that mindfulness yoga significantly reduces PTSD symptomatology and restores the homeostasis of the autonomic nervous system.

Van der Kolk explored various psychotherapies related to the brain, mind and body of PTSD patients. He emphasized the human body as the means of communicating with oneself and others and has suggested expressive therapies that make use of language, art, music and dance.

Ruella Frank, founder and director of the Center for Somatic Studies, NYC, and faculty at Gestalt Associates for Psychotherapy, has explored an important aspect of embodiment: movement in infancy and its relationship to adult experience. She is the author of articles and chapters in various publications, as well as several books including *Body of Awareness: A Somatic and Developmental Approach to Psychotherapy* (2001). The book introduces what she has come to call "the six fundamental movements," which are co-created within the infant/parent dyad in the first year of life and function within adult relationships. Frank has worked with these fundamental movements since 1976 when she was first introduced to the work of Bonnie Bainbridge-Cohen. Since that time, she has been continuing to develop and advance a present-centered, nonlinear and phenomenological developmental theory for Gestalt therapy.

Frank and Frances La Barre, a psychologist/psychoanalyst, have written *The First Year and the Rest of Your Life: Movement, Development and*

Psychotherapeutic Change (2010). They contend that the movement repertoire that develops in the first year of life is a language in itself and conveys desires, intentions and emotions. This early life in motion serves as the roots of ongoing nonverbal interaction and later verbal expression – in short, this language remains a key element in communication throughout life. They demonstrate how observations of fundamental movement interactions between babies and parents cue us to co-constructed experiences that underlie psychological development. Numerous clinical vignettes and detailed case studies show how movement observation opens the door to understanding problems that develop in infancy, and also those that appear in the continuing nonverbal dimension of adult communication. Their nonverbal lexicon, foundational movement analysis, enhances perception of emerging interactive patterns of parents and their babies, couples and individual adults within psychotherapy.

In *Bodily Roots of Experience in Psychotherapy: Moving Self* (2022) Frank explores the significance of movement processes as they shape experience throughout life. She introduces a new paradigm in the making of experience through an investigation into the basics of animated life. She contends that subverbal interactions form the foundation of lived experience. The centrality of these interactions to the therapeutic encounter is set forth through therapy vignettes. She examines the building of experience in infant-parent dyads and the functional similarity of those dyads to the unfolding patient-therapist relationship.

We now turn to the writings that contemporary psychoanalysts who have attempted to employ an embodied perspective often cite. A major contribution to embodiment in psychoanalysis was offered by Daniel Stern, who coined the term "vitality affects" (1985) and later "forms of vitality" (2010). Vitality affects or forms of vitality are, according to Stern, ever-changing feeling shapes reflecting the intensity, strength and rapidity of interaction. According to Stern:

> They are the felt experience of force – in movement – with a temporal contour, and a sense of aliveness, of going somewhere. They do not belong to any particular content. They are more form than content. They concern the "How," the manner, and the style, not the "What" or the "Why."
>
> (Stern, 2010, p. 8)

Stern and The Boston Change Process Study Group (2007) have provided a detailed account of embodiment. They contend that bodily emotional interaction constitutes the foundational level of our minds. They note that "previous psychoanalytic theory had the surface/depth distinction upside down" (2007, p. 2). "What has arisen from the previous upside-down view of the mind is a privileging of abstraction over interaction, a privileging of the symbolic/semantic over the affective/interactive" (p. 3). They add that "thinking itself requires and depends upon feeling emanating from the body, as well as upon movements and actions" (p. 12, 2007).

Another psychoanalyst who has developed a view of the mind as embodied is Armando Bianco Ferrari. In his book, *From the Eclipse of the Body the Dawn of Thought* (2004), he hypothesizes that the body is fundamental to the birth and development of mental functions. He observes:

> The human being cannot be regarded as capable of thought but devoid of emotion. . . . Emotions are part of the essential nature of thought. Furthermore, they originate the capacity for thought."
>
> (Ferrari, 2004, p. 33)

Riccardo Lombardi (2017; 2019) is also a prominent analyst who has emphasized the body. He writes:

> [I]t's hard to believe that an analysis can result in any sort of change if it is conducted at a purely intellectual level – that is, if it does not expand to involve the body and concrete action in real life.
>
> (Lombardi, 2017, p. 45)

Body-mind dissociation is Lombardi's central concept. Describing his book, he notes that it focuses attention in psychoanalysis on the body and the body-mind relationship, together with the conflict and dissociation that is sometimes found there.

> It involves taking note of a whole series of clinical phenomena characterized by a discordant arrangement, including the situation in which body and mind tend not to interact, but instead to exclude each other. Body and mind differ in their natures, hence we are all exposed, by the very nature of things, to a conflict between something concrete and something immaterial.
>
> (Lombardi, 2017, p. 1)

In contrast to seeing body and mind as differing in their nature, Roger Frie (2008) underscores that mind and self-experience are fundamentally embodied and intertwined with the social world. He states that "reflective thought is possible only as a result of our prereflective bodily sensations. Our bodily sensations form the basis for reflective thought and action" (2008, p. 373).

We would like to mention two more books published in the last ten years that strongly argue for embodying psychoanalysis. One is by the German analyst M. Leuzinger-Bohleber, who published the book *Finding the Body in the Mind: Embodied Memories, Trauma, and Depression* (2015), and the other is by the British analyst, Allesandra Lemma, who wrote *Minding the Body: The Body in Psychoanalysis and Beyond* (2014).

In 2022 we had the pleasure of editing a special issue of *Psychoanalytic Inquiry* entitled "The Turn Toward Embodiment" (Brothers & Sletvold, 2022a), which offered a variety of perspectives on embodiment. In addition to our own contribution *Talking Bodies: A New Vision of Psychoanalysis* (Brothers & Sletvold, 2022b), the issue features essays by

- Donnel B. Stern (2022) "Feels Like Me: Formulating the Embodied Mind."
- Siri Erika Gullestad (2022) "Finding the Mind in the Body."
- William F. Cornell (2022) "Wishing I Weren't Here: Therapeutic Engagement with Disembodied States."
- Gianni Nebbiosi & Susanna Federici (2022) "Miming and Clinical Psychoanalysis: Enhancing Our Intersubjective Sensibility."
- Steven H. Knoblauch (2022) "The Body as Subject, Intersubject, Fluid, and Reticular: A Series of Considerations Coming from Different Models."

We provide brief summaries of these articles, which we base on the authors' abstracts, to demonstrate the unique perspectives of these prominent contributors to the embodiment of psychoanalysis.

Reflecting on the invitation to contribute to the issue on embodiment, D. B. Stern mentions realizing that he had never explicitly addressed the subject. Choosing not to contextualize his thoughts about embodiment in the large, existing literature on the topic, he begins instead to think through the relation of embodiment to the phenomena he has described over the course of the last 40 years or so: *unformulated experience, dissociation, enactment* and *the interpersonal field*. He then takes up the relation of the verbal and the nonverbal, arguing that to grant a fundamental role to the body in psychoanalysis does not imply that language is secondary. He goes on to present an understanding of the role of embodied processes in the formulation of experience and ends with an illustration of somatic life in clinical process.

Siri Gullestad opens her contribution by stating that embodiment represents a new theoretical development and innovative research perspective within cognitive science and the philosophy of mind, emphasizing the important role that the body has in shaping the mind. She goes on to remind readers that the idea of the interconnection of mind and body is an old one and has long roots within psychoanalysis, particularly in the character-analytic tradition in which the "how" of relating and talking as expressed in nonverbal behavior and body language is emphasized. Her paper also explores how the patient's embodied, structuralized bearing and bodily appearance reveal relational messages. Through a case presentation, Gullestad illustrates how embodied affects and ways-of-being are actualized in the transference and can be captured through the embodied emotional response of the analyst. She contends that the concept of "relational scenarios" is fruitful for observing transference-countertransference dynamics.

William F. Cornell offers two clinical vignettes to illustrate the use of somatic receptivity and interventions in his bodily-based psychotherapy of patients experiencing severe levels of disembodiment. Drawing upon the work of Lombardi, Alvarez, and Bucci, he stresses the therapist's primary attention to mind-body splits (the vertical axis), in contrast to interpersonal/transference interpretations (the horizontal axis), in the treatment of chronic disembodied defenses.

Gianni Nebbiosi and Susi Federici elaborate on their conviction that one cannot study the human soul as "a thing," such that a discourse in the *third person* will never equate to a discourse in the *first person*. They contend that not all human communication is understandable and translatable into conceptual thought. They illustrate this assumption in a review of research that led them to their particular "technique" of miming after the session and explain this technique in some detail. What first seemed possible, they now consider essential: to have a therapeutic approach that would facilitate and deepen the communicative experience of two "acting bodies" in relation with one other. They call this procedure "mimetic understanding" because it provides an understanding based more on emotions and actions and less on conceptual thinking. They acknowledge their debt to Daniel Stern (particularly his concept of "vitality affects"), to Jessica Benjamin's notion of the *rhythmic third*, and to all the studies on infancy research that point to rhythm as the first form of meaning (Sander, Stern, Beebe, Knoblauch and many others).

Steven Knoblauch presents a reticular model of embodied subjectivity as an expansion of earlier hydraulic, plastic and resonant models. Three vignettes taken from early life experience serve to illustrate how a reticular model recontextualizes the processes represented in earlier models. He demonstrates how unconscious emotional experience emerges from a continuously fluid register of multimodal embodied experience in interaction with a particular socially ordering context, offering categories and hierarchies that can valorize or abject. Knoblauch argues that applying this model to the experiences described in the vignettes raises questions and possibilities for how intersectional categories and hierarchies of power emerge from and are shaped by the interaction of body and social context.

Summary

We hope this overview provides a sampling of the rich variety of perspectives that contribute to the embodiment of psychoanalysis. For a further review of the history of embodied psychoanalysis see *The Embodied Analyst – From Freud and Reich to Relationality* (Sletvold, 2014).

References

Boston Change Process Study Group. (2007). The foundational level of psychodynamic meaning: Implicit process in relation to conflict, defense, and the dynamic unconscious. *International Journal of Psychoanalysis, 88,* 1–16.

Brothers. D., & Sletvold, J. (Eds) (2022a). The turn toward embodiment. *Psychoanalytic Inquiry, 42,* 4.

Brothers, D., & Sletvold, J. (2022b). Talking bodies: A new vision of psychoanalysis. *Psychoanalytic Inquiry, 42*(4), 289–302.

Cornell, W. F. (2022). Wishing i weren't here: Therapeutic engagement with disembodied states. *Psychoanalytic Inquiry, 42*(4), 253–265.

Damasio, A. R. (1994/1995). *Descartes' error.* New York: Avon Books.

Ferrari, A. B. (2004). *From the eclipse of the body the dawn of thought.* London, England: Free Association Books.

Frank, R. (2001). *Body of awareness: A somatic and developmental approach to psychotherapy.* New York: GestaltPress.

Frank, R. (2022). *Bodily roots of experience in psychotherapy.* New York and London: Routledge.

Frank, R., & La Barre, F. (2010). *The first year and the rest of your life: Movement, development and psychotherapeutic change.* New York and London, England: Routledge.

Freud, S. (1890/1905). Psychical (or mental) treatment. In J. Strachey (Ed. & Trans.), *The standard edition of the complete psychological works of sigmund freud* (Vol. 7, pp. 283–302). London, England: The Hogarth Press, 1953.

Freud, S. (1923/1961). The ego and the id. In J. Strachey (Ed. & Trans.), *The standard edition of the complete psychological works of Sigmund Freud* (Vol. 19, pp. 1–66). London, England: The Hogarth Press.

Frie, R. (2008). Fundamentally embodied: The experience of psychological agency. *Contemp Psychoanal, 44*(3), 367–376.

Gullestad, S. E. (2022). Finding the mind in the body. *Psychoanalytic Inquiry, 42*(4), 244–252.

Knoblauch, S. H. (2022). The body as subject, intersubject, fluid, and reticular: A series of considerations coming from different models. *Psychoanalytic Inquiry, 42*(4), 278–288.

Lemma, A. (2014). *Minding the body – The body in psychoanalysis and beyond.* London, England and New York: Routledge Taylor & Frances.

Leuzinger-Bohleber, M. (2015). *Finding the body the mind. Embodied memories, trauma, and depression.* London, England: Karnac Books.

Levine, P. (1997). *Waking the tiger: Healing trauma: The innate capacity to transform overwhelming experiences.* Berkeley, CA: North Atlantic Books.

Levine, P. (2008). *Healing trauma: A pioneering program for restoring the wisdom of your body.* London: Sounds True, Inc.

Levit, D. (2018). Somatic experiencing: In the realm of trauma and dissociation – What we can do, when what we do, is really not good enough, *Psychoanalytic Dialogues, 28,* 586–601.

Lombardi, R. (2017). *Body-mind dissociation in psychoanalysis.* London, England and New York: Routledge Taylor and Frances Group

Lombardi, R. (2019). Developing a capacity for bodily concern: Antonio Damasio and the psychoanalysis of body-mind relationships. *Psychoanalytic Inquiry, 39*(8), 534–544.

Masson, J. M. (Ed. & Trans.) (1985). *The complete letters of Sigmund Freud to Wilhelm Flies: 1887–1904.* Cambridge, MA: Harward University Press.

Merleau-Ponty, M. (1945/1996). *Phenomenology of perception.* London, England and New York: Routledge.

Nebbiosi, G., & Federici, S. (2022). Miming and clinical psychoanalysis: Enhancing our inter-subjective sensibility. *Psychoanalytic Inquiry*, *42*(4), 266–277.

Reich, W. (1933/1949/1972). *Character analysis*. New York: Farrar, Straus and Giroux.

Sletvold, J. (2014) *The embodied analyst – From Freud and reich to relationality*. London, England and New York: Routledge Taylor & Frances.

Stern, D. B. (2022). Feels like me: Formulating the embodied mind. *Psychoanalytic Inquiry*, *42*(4), 244–252.

Stern, D. N. (1985). *The interpersonal world of the infant: A view from psychoanalysis and developmental psychology*. New York: Basic Books

Stern, D. N. (2010). *Forms of vitality. Exploring dynamic experience in psychology, the arts, psychotherapy, and development*. Oxford: Oxford University Press.

Van der Kolk, B. A. (Ed.) (1984). *Post-traumatic stress disorder: Psychological and biological sequelae*. Washington, DC: American Psychiatric.

Van der Kolk, B. A. (1987). *Psychological trauma*. Washington, DC: American Psychiatric.

Van der Kolk, B. A. (2014). *The body keeps the score: Brain, mind and body in the healing of trauma*. New York: Viking.

Van der Kolk, B. A., McFarlane, A. C., & Weisaeth, L. (Eds.) (1996). *Traumatic stress: The effects of overwhelming experiences on mind, body and society*. New York: Guilford.

Index

abuse, suffering 45
adult-onset traumatic experiences 32
affective languages/rhythms/relations, production 22
affective process, involvement 22
affective translation, understanding 22
affect regulation 63
alcohol: addiction 100–101; influence 103
Alexander, Franz 88
anaclitic depression 90
anal development phase (Freud theory) 29
analysis: emotional process 106–107; goal, change 41
Analysis of the Self, The (Kohut) 88
analysis, seeking (reason) 91
analyst, patient perception 97
analytic meetings, acknowledgment 21–22
analytic treatment, benefit (absence) 62–63
Anderson, Sam 87–88
anger, absence 45, 98
anonymity, psychoanalytic standards 90
anorexia, suffering 35
antidepressant medication, need 58
anxiety 59, 73
Arendt, Hannah 69, 70
Aron, Lewis 75, 97
Asperger, Hans 62
Asperger syndrome 62–63
asymmetrical relationship, patient formation 76–77
attention-deficit hyperactive disorder (ADHD) 7, 30, 55, 61, 96; diagnoses 60; female adult ADHD 61
attention, longing 46
attention, usage 99
attunement, impact 22
auditory hallucinations 45
authenticity, usage 99

autism spectrum 62–63
autobiography, draft (change) 17
awareness, conscious/unconscious levels 28

back rubs, usage 93
Beebe, Beatrice 16
behavioral therapy, impact 99
being (modes), self-state (compatibility) 43
Bell's palsy, impact 51, 53
Benjamin, Jessica 117
Bettleheim, Bruno 62–63
blurring, impact 22
bodily basis, establishment 110
bodily communications, monitoring 15
bodily ego (Freud) 9
bodily experience, contact 13
bodily I, I (relationship) 12
bodily movements, synchronicity (absence) 58–59
Bodily Roots of Experience in Psychotherapy (Frank) 114
bodily sensations, touch 33
body: alienation 87–88; differences 94; dualism 88; feeling 80; focus, neurobiologically based models (usage) 112; holding 21; human relationship 87; patient focus 112; relaxed feeling 23; talking 16–17, 96; transcendence 93–94
body-based psychoanalysis 10
body-based supervision 78
body-based theory 110
Body Keeps the Score, The (van der Kolk) 112
body-mind dissociation 115
Body of Awareness (Frank) 113
body-self, references 8
body-to-body exchanges, usage 14–15
body-to-body feeling connection 57; requirement 57

body-to-body, gross disturbances 30
bone-thin fantasy 37
Boston Change Process Study Group 41;
    embodiment account 114–115
Brandchaft, Bernard 30
Bromberg, Philip 6, 43
Brothers, Doris 27; patient (Amy)
    interaction 22; patient (Ben) interaction
    71; patient (Grace) interaction 92;
    patient (Jen) interaction 57; patient
    (Lyle) interaction 63; patient (Marcia)
    interaction 35; patient (Tina) interaction
    91; patient (Tracy) interaction 51; story
    1–3
Buber, Martin 75, 77
burnout, symptoms 61
Bystanders No More (conference) 5

caregivers, modelling 29
castration 102
Catay, Zeynep 8, 93
Center for Somatic Studies 113
changed priorities 74
change, freedom: absence 7, 55;
    constitutional factors 59–60
change, resistance 60
Character Analysis (Reich) 111
character-analytic experiences, impact 69
character neurosis, phrase (usage) 30
character, term (usage) 30
chest, tightness (feeling) 36
childhood: masturbation 107; sexual
    traumas, accounting 102
clinical experience, knowledge 29
clinical interactions, description 65
clinical phenomena 115
closeness, maintenance 59
collectiveness, valuation 29
communication: empathic communication
    64; style 31–32
compassion 73
competition, terror 84
complexity-reducing efforts 38
concept-based language 10
concept-based theory 110
confidence, winning 99–100
confrontation, seeking 106
connectedness, feeling 85
conscious awareness, I-you-we-world flow
    (unavailability) 15
conscious memory: dissociation 56; role 49
consciousness, experience 15
constitutional factors 96

contempt, re-experiencing 85
copulation, picture 101–102
Cornell, William F. 5, 90, 116
co-transferences 50
counter-transferences 50
COVID crisis, impact 37, 58, 69, 93
cultural pressures 98
cultural process, involvement 22
cultural translation, need 22

Damasio, Antonio R. 17, 57
Dear Zealots (Oz) 75
deceleration 28
declarative memory 49, 50
delusions 35
Demons in the Consulting Room
    (Harris, et al.) 38
depression 52, 59
dialogues, maintenance 75
discomfort, feeling 100
disfiguring illness, impact 51
disregard, re-experiencing 85
disruption, creation 86
dissociated experience, focus (shift) 42
dissociated mental content, release 40
dissociation 116; embodied understanding
    46; embodiment 40; interpersonalization
    40; traumatic dissociation, clinical
    examples 37–38
dissociative forgetting 48
dissociative measures 30
dissociative mental content,
    understanding 40
dissociative processes, links 43
Doolittle, Hilda: experience 103–105;
    Freud meeting 103–104
Door-Keeper 104
dream, interpretation (Freud) 101
dyad, joint directionality (fittedness) 41

early traumatic experiences 32
ego: bodily ego, equivalence 9; Freud
    perception 9; ideal 98
either/or relationship 35
Ellis, Havelock 104
embarrassment, overwhelming 105
Embodied Analyst, The (Sletvold) 4
embodied connectedness: failures,
    countering 37; feeling 41
embodied connecting, influence 48
embodied dialogues, us vs. them alternative
    74–75
embodied history 17

embodied language 9
embodied narratives 50
embodied relating, mutual sense
    (development) 58
embodied stories 16–17
embodied supervision 3
embodied we-connectedness, basis 75
embodied wholeness, emergence 42
embodiment: analyst focus 1; aspects,
    understanding 24; imagination,
    relationship 35; past/present views 110
emotion, absence 115
emotional challenges 28
emotional distance 52
emotional neglect 25
empathic communication 64
empathy: efforts 85; expression 98; path,
    imitation (usage) 12
enactments 48, 116; dissolving, absence 41;
    term, avoidance 42
energy-discharge science, Freud reliance 7–8
erotic transferences 50
Escape from Freedom (Fromm) 68
experience: reflection, willingness 73; self-
    with-other method 43; transformation 41
expression: display 21; understanding 12
expressive movements, imitation
    (creation) 12

faces, expressions (display) 21
facial expressions, echoing 25
facial muscles, tensions/relaxations 9
failing, dread 57
Falling Backwards (Brothers) 2
false connection, usage 49–50
familiar/unfamiliar, interplay 20
fanatic, defining 75
fantasy 82; bone-thin fantasy 37;
    intensification 32
fascist experience, us-them binary 68
fascistic we 70
fascist leaders, relationships
    (similarities) 68
father: fear 102; relationship, sweetness
    (recapture) 91
faulty reasoning 65
Federici, Susanna 5, 116
female adult ADHD 61
Ferrari, Armando Bianco 115
Finding the Body in the Mind (Leuzinger-
    Bohleber) 115
first person discourse 117

First Year and the Rest of Your Life (La Barre/
    La Barre) 113–114
force, felt experience 114
foreign bodies, interpretation/translation 20
"foreign bodies" psychoanalytic
    encounters 6
foreignness, encounters 20
forms of vitality 114
Fosshage, James 17
Foucault, Michel 76
Frank, Ruella 3, 113–114
Frederick, Ann 111
Freud, Sigmund: challenge,
    intuition (usage) 104–105; Doolittle
    experience 103–105; Doolittle meeting
    103–104; implied criticism 105;
    interpretation, initiation 101; regret
    108; theoretical understanding 102;
    Wolf-Man, experience 99–103; wordless
    challenge 105
Frie, Roger 7, 14, 56, 115
Fromm, Eric 68, 97; experience 105–107;
    face-to-face encounter, offering 106;
    personal encounter 106
From Psychoanalysis to Orgone Biophysics
    (Reich) 111
From the Eclilpse of the Body the Dawn of
    Thought (Ferrari) 115
fundamental movements 17
Funk, Rainer (Fromm experience) 105–107

gaze, hostage (feeling) 51–52
Gestalt Associates for Psychotherapy 113
gestures, echoing 25
going-on-being 55
grief 92
guilt, feelings 58
Gullestad, Siri Erika 5, 116

handshake, reaction 90
Harris, Adrienne 38
healing, shared venture 53
here-and-now problems 25
high-functioning autism 30, 55, 62–64
History Beyond Trauma (Davoine/
    Guadilliere) 76
history, making (location) 14
History of Sexuality, The (Foucault) 76–77
Hitler, ideology (exploration) 70
Hitlerjugend 74
Holocaust: societal trauma 76; survivors 58
hospitalism 90

human bodies, interaction 11
human embodiment: impact 11; sense 89
human encounter, newness 106
humor, usage 99
Hustvedt, Siri 13
hybridity 22
hypnosis 90
hysteria 108; treatment 90

I: bodily I, relationship 12; experience,
    integration 42; experiencing 44; flow
    (limitation), binaries (impact) 30; focus
    43–44; supervisory position 7; world,
    impact 14
icebox mothers, blame 63
I-centered, becoming 48
I-centered body, dissociative reactions
    (revealing) 30
I-centeredness 56; domination 70; impact
    44; intensity, focus 60; result 30
I-centeredness, development 6;
    constitutional factors, role 29–30
I-centered patients, resemblance 60
I-centered person 43–44
idealizing transference 53
I-experiences, variety 44
imagination: embodiment, relationship 35;
    intensification 32
imitation: creation, movements (impact) 12;
    power, awareness (Freud) 12
implicit memory 49, 50
individuals, Cartesian view 56
infantile neurosis 102
inner world, Fromm (connection) 105–106
in-person sessions 22–23
insomnia, suffering 84
interhuman (Buber) 75
internal perception 110–111
International Association of Psychoanalytic
    Self Psychology (IAPSP) 76
International Association of Relational
    Psychanalysis and Psychotherapy
    (IARPP) 76
interpenetrating flow, physical appearance
    (impact) 60
interpersonal field 116
interpersonal relationships, emotional
    conflicts 73
interpretation: conception 20; cultural
    systems 17
intersubjectivity 10
intimacy 81; usage 99

Introductory Lectures in Psychoanalysis
    (Freud) 3
I position 16, 78; Doris patient 23, 36, 52,
    58, 65, 72; Jon patient 25, 33, 45, 61, 73;
    supervision session 80, 82, 85
irony, usage 99
I, word usage: connection 12; rationale 5
I-you-we: design 78; positions, completion
    79; world, interaction 96
I-you-we-world: body-based sensing
    42; breakdown 6; communication
    27; complexity 15; deceleration 6;
    freezing 51; intermingling flow 43;
    interpenetrating flow, physical appearance
    (impact) 60; maintenance, body-to-body
    exchanges (usage) 14–15; organization,
    bodily communications (monitoring) 15;
    shared flow, emergence 22; totality 14
I-you-we-world flow 5, 14–15; attainment,
    difficulty 28; complexity 14–15;
    component, emphasis/focus 48,
    49; consciousness/unconsciousness,
    relationship 15; deceleration, fixations
    (combination) 29; development 108;
    disruptions 7, 27, 40–41, 43–44,
    57; experience, absence 32; fluidity/
    effortlessness, rarity 28, 60, 96; fluidity,
    increase 24; impact 15; intermingling 16,
    28, 46, 96; interweaving 28; interweaving,
    resumption 53; reinstatement 54;
    slowing/freezing 6, 56; slow motion
    movement 51; trauma-generated
    disturbances 29; trauma, impact 15;
    traumatic experience, emphasis 29;
    unavailability 15; uniqueness 79

joint directionality, fittedness
    (development) 41

Kanner, Leo 62
Klein, George 10
Knausgaard, Karl Ove 70
Knoblauch, Steven H. 5, 116
Kohut, Heinz 29, 55, 88–89
Kuchuck, Steven 98

La Barre, Frank/Frances 113–114
Lachmann, Frank 17
language: social activity 70; treatment
    (Merleau-Ponty) 11
latent negative transference 57
Lemma, Allesandra 115

Leuzinger-Bohleber, M. 115
Levinas, Emanuel 77
Levine, Peter 27, 111–112
Levit, David 112
life: body/concrete action, involvement 115;
    dreams, focus 80; experiences, impact 13;
    repugnance 53
linguistic process, involvement 22
lion-like creature, approach 104
liquid times 69
lives, shape (understandability) 17
Lombardi, Riccardo 115
love, longing 46
LSD, use 94

Maduro, Peter 28
man, states of mind (manifestation) 9
marriage, agreement 85
Mass Psychology of Fascism, The (Reich) 69
masturbation: attention 108; childhood
    masturbation 107; sadomasochistic
    pornographic videos, usage 65
maternal transferences 50
McFarlane, Alexander C. 112
Mein Kampf (Hitler) 70
memory 4; aspects 49–50; dynamic process
    49; emergence, input 34; flooding 36;
    importance 6; role 49; vulnerability 45
mental functions, birth/development 115
mental illness, concept 76–77
mentalization 10
mentalizing 63
Merleau-Ponty, Maurice 11, 14, 111
Metaphors We Live By (Lakoff/Johnson) 11
#metoo movement, rise 90
mind-body-self, experience 88
mind, clarification 60
mindfulness yoga, impact 113
Minding the Body (Lemma) 115
modelling, occurrence 38
modern life, exit 100
moral neutrality 74–75
movements: echoing 25; synchrony 34
multiple self-states 40, 43–44; concept,
    replacement 44
My Recollections of Sigmund Freud
    (Wolf-Man) 99

narrative 17, 48; creation 21
National Socialists (Nazis), rally speeches 75
Nazism, abhorrence 74
Nebbiosi, Gianni 5, 116

needs, one-sided adaptation 33
neglect, suffering 45
neurotic styles, phrase (usage) 30
neutrality, psychoanalytic standards 90
New Language for Psychoanalysis, A
    (Schafer) 10
non-gratification, psychoanalytic
    standards 90
nonsexual touch 91
nonverbal communication, body
    alignment 32
non-we, dehumanization/expulsion 70
Norwegian Character Analytic
    Institute 7, 78
Novak, Edward 91

objective resemblance 11
object relations 10
oedipal transferences 50
one-person drive theory 88
onomatopoetic theory 11
oral development phase (Freud theory) 29
Orange, Donna 75
other, nonverbal perception 41
Oz, Amos 75

pain, avoidance 53
paranoid preoccupations 35
partners, directions (coordination) 41
passiveness, characterization 92
past disruptions, repetition 46
past traumas, revival 28
paternal transferences 50
patient heads, Freud (touching) 90
Patient's Experience of the Analyst's
    Subjectivity, The (Aron) 97
people, presence 89
periodic distress 58
personal therapy, reference 99
Pesso Boyden System Psychomotor Therapy
    (PBSP) 4
phallic development phase (Freud theory) 29
Philosophy in the Flesh (Lakoff/Johnson)
    11–12
phonemes, singing 11
physical embodiment 38–39
Physical Touch in Psychoanalytic Psychotherapy
    (Novak) 91
political disagreements 73
political malevolence 69
positive feeling, verbalization 92
posttraumatic experiential modes 56

post-traumatic stress disorder (PTSD) 111–113; model, difficulty 27–28; symptoms 32
Post-traumatic Stress Disorder (van der Kolk) 112
prelinguistic/linguistic phases, gap 11
"processes of thought" 110
psychedelic substances, use 94
psychoanalysis: embodiment 110–111; emotional processes 106–107; us/them, involvement 75–77
psychoanalytic dialogues, conducting 96
psychoanalytic healing 96
psychoanalytic theory: future 5–8; present status 5
psychoanalytic treatment 112; resistance 59–60
psychobiology 88
psychological survival 4–5, 56
Psychological Trauma (van der Kolk) 112
psychological understanding, absence 100
psychology: bodily basis, establishment 110; organic basis, absence 110
psychoneuroses, aetiology 102
psychopath, impact 103
psychotherapy, bodily basis (establishment) 110
pure psychology 88

racial difference, effects 52
racism 69
radical loneliness 69
Reich, Wilhelm 7, 9, 12, 57, 69, 88, 111
Relational Concepts in Psychoanalysis (Mitchell) 4
relationship, development 65
Representations of Interactions (RIGs) 17
resistance 7, 55, 59–60; force, reduction 70
rhythmic third 117
Rogerian Client-Centered therapy 4
romantic connection, establishment 25–26

Sachs, Hanns 103, 104
sadistic satisfaction 103
sadomasochistic pornographic videos, usage 65
Sauvayre, Pascal 14
Schafer, Roy 10, 50
schizophrenia, diagnosis 45
Schjelderup, Harald 106
secret resistance 57
seduction, theory 102

self: contact, loss 60; genetic interpretation 89
self-awareness, limitation 97
self-control, difficulties 61
self-diagnosis, confirmation 32
self-disclosure, focus 97
self-disturbances 89
self-involved parents, neglect 31
self-loathing 35
self-object transferences 50
self-states, being modules 43
Seven Little Goats, The (fairy tale) 102
sexism 69
sexual abuse 25; theory 102
sexual drives, repression 107
sexual excitement, feeling 107–108
sexual experiences, significance 102
sexual molestation 91
shame, feelings 58
Shattered Self, The (Ulman) 2
Signs (Merleau-Ponty) 11
"silence between the words" 5–6
sister, seduction 101
skin problem 89–91
skin-to-skin contact 89
Sletvold, Jon 16; patient (Laura) interaction 44; patient (Lynn) interaction 60; patient (Maya) interaction 24; patient (Peter) interaction 32; patient (Tom) interaction 73; story 3–5, 24–25
Smith, Zadie 21
social language 63
societal antagonism 53
societal trauma 76
soft-hearted-soft-headed approach 71
Somatic Experiencing (SE) 111
somatic processes, connection 110
somatic symptoms 72
Speech, movement 14
Spitz, Rene 90
splitting 40–41
Stanley, Jason 68, 75
Stern, Daniel 17, 114
Stern, Donnel B. 5, 6, 41, 46, 116
Stilson, Kathy 2
Strand, Nils 4
Studies on Hysteria (Freud/Breuer) 49, 50, 102
subtle neurological conditions 55
sugar binging 91
Sullivan, Harry Stack 56
supervision, conducting 79

supervision session: Chinese therapists,
    involvement 83–84; examples 80, 81;
    group responses 81, 83, 85–86; patients
    (Li/Sue) 84–85; usage 84

Talking Bodies: A New Vision of Psychoanalysis
    (Brothers/Sletvold) 116
talking cure (Freud) 90
temporal process, involvement 22
them: impact 75–77; meanings 76
theoretical understanding (Freud) 102
theories, importance 107–108
therapeutic dyad, expectations (creation) 41
therapeutic process, description 16
therapeutic relationship: memory, aspects
    49–50; progress 78; us-them binary
    domination 75
therapist: patient perception, importance
    98–99; patient relationship 99
Third Reich, atrocities 70
Thought, movement 14
Thoughts for the times on War and Death
    (Freud) 14
tones of voice, echoing 25
touch: importance 93; negative
    consequences 89–90; sexual connotations,
    fears 90
Toward a Psychology of Uncertainty
    (Brothers) 2, 4
transference: embodied connectedness 51;
    occurrence, false connection (usage) 49
transference, embodiment 48
transgression, fear 83
translation, word (roots) 22
transparent wall 81
trauma 4; aftermath 59–60; analyst
    treatment, question 38–39; context 43;
    experience 27; transmission 38;
    treatment, non-psychoanalytic
    approaches 112
trauma-generated disturbances 29
trauma-generated narrative, sharing 53
traumatic dissociation, clinical examples
    37–38
traumatic experience: emphasis 29;
    revival 42–43
Traumatic Stress (van der Kolk/McFarlane/
    Weisaeth) 112
traumatized bodies 27
traumatized/traumatizing world 96
treatment, ending (question) 83
trophy wife, husband wish 24

Trump, Donald: far-right conspiracies 71;
    fascistic strategies 74–75; fascist-leaning
    leader 68; witch hunt, reaction 72

Ulman, Richard 2, 27
unconscious memory, role 49
unconscious memory-traces 101–102
unconsciousness, experience 15
unformulated experience 116
upright posture, stiffness 36
us: impact 75–77; patient perceptions,
    validation/confirmation 97; world
    explosion 14
us-them binary 7, 62; domination 75; fascist
    experience 68; vulnerability 96; we,
    transformation 44
us-them connectedness 70
us-them stance 71
"us *vs.* them" 70; embodied dialogues,
    alternative 74–75

van der Kolk, Bessel 27, 112–113
verbal assault 45
verbal communication: body alignment 32;
    experience, transformation 41
verbalizations, impact 30–31, 36
vitality affects 114, 117
voice, modulation 21
vowels, singing 11

Waking the Tiger: Healing Trauma (Levine) 111
we: basis 70; connectedness, unifying sense
    (absence) 76; experiencing 44; focus
    43–44; supervisory position 7; word
    usage, rationale 5; world, impact 14
we-centered body, dissociative reactions
    (revealing) 30
we-centeredness: development 6;
    extreme forms, emergence 30; extreme
    forms, exemplification 31; reasons,
    understanding 32; result 30
we-connectedness 29; embodied sense,
    development 56; embodiment 57;
    enhancement 57; sense,
    impoverishment 30
we-connection, formation 74
we, experience: life experiences, impact 13;
    transformation 44
we flow (limitation), binaries (impact) 30
Weisaeth, Lars 112
we-ness: change 70; embodied sense 77;
    varieties 13

we-ness, sense: body-to-body feeling connection, requirement 57; development 7; quality 15; violence 30

we position 16, 79; Doris patient 23, 37, 53, 59, 66, 72; Jon patient 25, 34, 46, 61, 74; supervision session 81, 83, 85

we, sense 29; creation ability, damage 70; dependence 13; emergence 46

whiteness, contrast 53

Wing, Lorna 62

Wolf-Man: experience 99–103; infantile neurosis 102; peace/quiet, feeling 100; problems, understanding 102–103

Women Against Rape 2

wordless challenge 105

words: finding 10–14; silence between 9, 16–17; singing 11

work, presentation 82

world: concept 14; concerns 68; experiencing 44; singing 11; word usage, rationale 5, 13

world, experience: constriction 30; gaining 84

"Writing on the Wall" (Doolittle) 103

xenophobia 69

you: being 106; experiences 13; experiences, integration 42; experiencing 44; focus 13, 43–44; supervisory position 7; world, impact 14

you-centered body, dissociative reactions (revealing) 30

you-centeredness 56; body communication 31; development 6; domination 70; result 30; traumatic origins 30; understanding 33

you-centered people, focus 48

you-centered relational style 33

you-centered style, development 33

you flow (limitation), binaries (impact) 30

you position 16; assuming 79; Doris patient 23, 36, 52, 59, 66, 72; Jon patient 25, 33, 46, 61, 74; supervision session 80, 82, 85

you, word usage: connection 12; rationale 5

Zoom sessions, usage 58, 80

For Product Safety Concerns and Information please contact our EU
representative GPSR@taylorandfrancis.com
Taylor & Francis Verlag GmbH, Kaufingerstraße 24, 80331 München, Germany

www.ingramcontent.com/pod-product-compliance
Lightning Source LLC
Chambersburg PA
CBHW050615280326
41932CB00016B/3056